I0441749

Ethics and the Earth

Missionary

OUTLINING STANDARDS FOR ECOPSYCHOLOGY AND MINDFULLY INHABITING THE EARTH

Tiffany A. Dedeaux, MA

Ethics And The Earth Missionary:
Outlining Standards For
Ecopsychology And Mindfully
Inhabiting The Earth

Written by Tiffany A. Dedeaux

© 2013 Tiffany A. Dedeaux

Inquiries should be addressed to

SACRED TIME™
103 E. Holly Street #407
Bellingham, WA 98225
SACRED-TIME.COM

ISBN-13: 978-1484869611
ISBN-10: 1484869613

ALSO BY TIFFANY A. DEDEAUX:

ROOTED IN WATER:
THE IMPORTANCE OF STORY TO ECOPSYCHOLOGY AND THE
BEGINNING OF A PRACTICE IN NARRATIVE ECOPSYCHOLOGY

Dedication

This book is dedicated to

You, *the curious, the reflective, the one who's aware and is trying to find your way.*

To

Mark *and* **Daisy**
who encourage me to dream big and be open enough to see the world differently.

And to
Betsy
who suggested I follow the bear.

Table of Contents

Acknowledgements

Preface

Why This Book...13

A Place to Start..14

Chapter 1:

Two Paths, One Destination 17

Chapter 2:

The Value and the Choice 28

Chapter 3:

Transformation and Insight...................41

Chapter 4:

Fresh Eyes 56

Chapter 5:

The Value of the Journey 75

References..84

Appendix...102

Acknowledgments

Ethics and the Earth Missionary is not only the journey of a student finding her way, it is also the maturing of a graduate walking that path. As this book is adapted from a paper I wrote while attending Antioch University in Seattle, I must first thank **Alexandra Hepburn** as she was the professor who read and commented on the original work. I must also thank **Lisa Reddick Lynch** for not only assigning the books that directed me to this path, but for editing the papers that have become a part of this quest. I want to acknowledge **Dominga Rosalita** for being herself. This alone has expanded my own thinking. She has inspired and given me feedback on my first work: *Rooted in Water*. She has also supported me as I navigated this one. In life, in thought, and in art, she encourages me to be my higher self.

I would also like to recognize **Mark**, **Daisy**, and **Anne** for supporting me as I began to explore how I would put this book together; **Stephanie** for helping me to find my voice; and **Betsy Hasegawa** for suggesting that I 'follow the bear.' I did and found an incredible windfall of inspiration that guided me along this journey and into the wilderness of understanding...

Preface

Ethics and the Earth Missionary is a pilgrimage that outlines what ethics could be in the study of the human/nature relationship, known as ecopsychology. This book, originally a graduate-level independent study assignment (Appendix A), is adapted with an evolving voice from a practical realization that as inhabitants of the earth a *code of conduct*, which I use interchangeably with *code of ethics* and *ethical standards*, is something for all of us to consider. Why? Because, based on my understanding of works like *Storms of My Grandchildren* by James Hansen, we are forcing the resilient earth we call home to adjust and change in ways that are not supportive of human life as we've known it,[1] and forcing ourselves out of house and home sooner than it would otherwise occur.

INSIDE A HURRICANE

In *Working Identity* by Herminia Ibarra, it is recognized that being in transition—as we are in relationship with the rest of the natural world—is to be in transit or in "voyage from one place to another."[2] For some, this transition could feel like "living inside a hurricane" because of a mix of feelings including "anticipation, confusion, [and] fear."[ii] We are transitioning from life as we've known it to a time when we cannot "avoid the devastating impact of raging fires, and crippling drought, and more powerful storms,"[iii] as President Barack Obama noted in his second inaugural address.[3]

Months after my first attempt at writing this section, the northeast coast of the United States experienced Superstorm Sandy. According to media coverage, it was the 'October surprise' of the 2012 presidential election season. In an interview on *The Rachel Maddow Show*,[4] New York Governor Andrew Cuomo indicated that rising water and climate change was no joke, and whether one subscribed to the science behind it or not, the effect was real. If a 'storm of the century' occurs annually—and destroys whole communities—it stands to reason that how we live and build will be affected by our changing climate. This brings the impact of climate change down from what's going on with the planet to what's going on with our region, our family.[iv]

Whether we intend to or not, we "co-create our lives from the interactions we have as a person-in-place."[5] Personally, I feel the most free to be myself at the place I call home. I refer to my neighborhood as the area around my home, where I have relationships with others. Equating place with relationship suggests that "the loss of place cuts into our experience of the continuity of life"[6] because what is important to us in terms of activities and people are held by these places. If those places change or no longer hold the people or activities that matter to us, we can experience 'homesickness.' The pain we feel when the place we love "is under immediate assault" is known as *Solastalgia*.[7]

In my look at *Ecopsychology and the Experience of Grief and Loss*,[8] I outline how we could live with what we know. Your emotional reaction to "environmental loss, damage, or destruction regardless of whether that change [was] brought about by human or natural causes," is real. You feel it whether you survived the storm or directly witnessed the aftermath. I suggested that the process we engage in to deal with these emotions include three stages:

1. ***Awareness and understanding for what we feel and are going through.*** This is so that we find the words to acknowledge what we're feeling or experiencing, as well as identify what is truly going on. An example of this could be Governor Cuomo admitting he no longer accepts that storms such as Sandy are "once in a lifetime," which is why he is looking at, in Maddow's words, "reimagining...the infrastructure that makes New York City possible."[4] This reimagining could include a building code that addresses repeated flooding by requiring the first floors of structures to house cars instead of people.

2. ***Recognizing and beginning to move forward with our relationship to the environment through ritual.*** The ritual can be of your own making, but I do suggest that it include some kind of literal or symbolic action that acknowledges what is dead and dying, celebrates what is living, and is repeated as part of a plan to move forward. If we consider this in relationship to the earth, then my idea is to create a program and make it a part of Earth Day so that we honor how far we've come in our understanding, while finding ways to keep Earth Day alive and relevant.[5] When considering the death of a loved one, I have a client who has moved from focusing on the death of her family member, to the celebration of an eventual spiritual reunion. She now marks the occasion with an intimate gathering of family and friends. On another level, a ritual recognizes what has been left behind and what will be gained in the process. When I fasted for

a life vision during the summer of 2010, I poured out my limited supply of water to symbolize letting go of the heartache of failure I was carrying around with me. I forgave myself aloud so that I could feel the words vibrate in my throat and hear them ring in my ears. Then I made a gesture through the air with my arm as a way of pulling back toward me the parts of myself that I had lost. Because that experience happened during Summer Solstice I hold some kind of vigil throughout the year to remind me of all that I learned on my quest. I call this my *soulstice* because the intent is to not stray far from my celestial center.

3. ***Receiving direction and a plan on how to address the situation.*** A plan will give you a course of action in addition to a sense of direction. It is also more likely to be impactful if it means something to you on a personal level. In *Changing for Good,*[9] James Prochaska, John Norcross, and Carlo Diclemente documented that change is a process that must begin with the recognition that there's a problem. If you don't see that there's a problem to be addressed, and you move into action on the insistence of others, you'll likely feel pushed and relapse back to a stage of contemplation.[v] Regardless of how you get there, change doesn't end with action. It must be maintained. Ritual can serve as both a reminder and a way to reinvigorate your commitment to change.

In *Rooted in Water*[10] I examined the relationship between slave descendants known as the Gullah Geechee and the environment of the Sea Islands. Marquetta 'Queen Quet' Goodwine, spokesperson for the Gullah Geechee Nation, would show her gratitude any time she arrived at the shores of the Atlantic Ocean. This was her way to "first give thanks to the Creator for allowing me to be able to hear and still touch." Her ritual of gratitude was also a way to "give homage to all of my ancestors who are still in that space," as well as a "prayer for the right energy to be conducted into the remaining meetings of the day." As we go about our busy lives, playing on the shores without recognizing the history in the soil, Queen Quet believes our ancestors are "going to rise up again and what other people recognize as a hurricane is going to wipe out a lot of what we see."[vi]

While I suggest that climate change is something to address rather than a threat from an invisible force out to harm us, President Obama has declared that "we will respond" because not doing so would mean we "betray our children and future generations."[3] As we consider how we conduct ourselves in light of our place in the generational timeline, it is fair to point out that there's a difference between what is ethical and what is moral, so we will explore a bit about both. As you consider how your relationship with nature has been and will be, I can appreciate how you might be transitioning between ways in which you identify yourself. You also might be moving from "letting go of the old or embracing the new" with the intent to "end up in a better position to make informed choices."[vii] Whatever we take or leave from this journey, I suggest that part of the plan be to share what we know so that those who will call us their ancestors can build from this point rather than rebuild to this point.

WHY THIS BOOK

 Ethics and the Earth Missionary is a supplement for those of you who are studying ethics or establishing your own personal code of conduct. This is a book based on the idea that we can take lessons learned from the treatment of indigenous people by some Christian missionaries, and apply it to our own treatment of native life as we, the human animal, move into wilderness territory. We are not the only ones who live and breathe in this environment, so it is not us *against* the natural world; it is us as a *part* of the natural world. While we'll look at what ecopsychologists can learn from Christian missionaries, I will also explore some Greek mythology because myths are important tools of connection that identify "patterns in human experience [and] address the problems we face."[7]

 As you join me on this journey, it is my hope that you don't have to be an academic to understand this text because this is a work comprised of story and metaphor intended to follow curiosity, increase our level of awareness, expand our perspective, and challenge us to consider what we should take into account as inhabitants of the earth. For those seeking additional information, you will find that the materials I cite or refer to are numbered to correspond with the source in the *References* section of this book.[1] The Roman numerals are used to correspond with the *Notes* section of this book for content that may need further explanation or context.[viii]

 If you're reading this, you may be curious about the insights that come from this pilgrimage, what you'll learn about yourself, and how you've been approaching your relationship with your environment. You might also be curious about the guidelines that you can adopt for the way you live and work. This book is meant for you, the curious, the reflective, the one who is aware and is trying to find your way.

A PLACE TO START

When I wrote the original paper (Appendix A), I sought and could not find anything that clearly laid out ethical standards for ecopsychology. Realizing that I could examine established interrelated fields—such as ecology, psychology, and environmentalism—I combed the internet for a code of ethics for each profession with the intent to include them in the Appendix (B, C, D). During the process I searched for ethics in the profession of conservation psychology and came across a section of the American Psychological Association website. It listed both conservation psychology and ecopsychology under *interest area*. This might suggest that the code of ethics that addresses the field of psychology would also address ecopsychology. While I'm willing to accept this, I think it is important to consider possible standards for ecopsychology specifically and then determine if the code for psychology is enough (See Chapter 5).

Creating a separate code of ethics or adding an addendum to psychology's established code would include the earth as part of the discourse as well as recognize the role of ecopsychology in questioning the entire system. Theodore Roszak, who coined the term *ecopsychology* in 1992, was first to use the term *counterculture* in 1968. With *counterculture* his intent was a call to rebel against "certain essential elements of industrial society."[11] With *ecopsychology* his intent was, in part, to create a new conversation between "scientific intellect and human need."[ix] He also intended the area of study to serve as a wakeup call for psychology, which, at its roots (See Chapter 1) was ecopsychology because it looked at the entirety of life.[12]

In our relationship with the rest of the natural world, the discovery of the 'New World' no longer refers to Christopher Columbus finding America. This is no longer a time when Europeans in search of paradise head west, [14] discover wilderness, and feel as though they have to fight for their survival.[x] The wilderness is also not here merely to "feed the souls" of the troubled or those labeled 'at-risk' as it seems with some wilderness therapy progams.[15] For ecopsychology, this relationship is not about looking at the rest of nature as a resource to be mined or an adversary to be fought, it is about recognizing the beauty of the natural world for the clarity and fresh perspective that comes with immersion, and how that connection appears vital to our overall well-being.[xi]

Follow the Bear

I roll over and there, silhouetted in the darkness of my tent is a bear. All I can make out is the outline of the head and immensely broad shoulders. I am unsure of how to respond but I don't feel threatened.

Eventually I fall asleep.

I am at a time of promise. I have been freed from all previous obligations and commitments and there is the chance of open, unrestricted, and creative time filling my schedule.

Promise is exciting.

My self-imposed scheduled prison has been holding me back. This morning I feel it more pronounced: it's time to write.

I rise and ready myself for a trek to Seattle. At the Fairhaven train station I sit on a bench and look down at my feet. Beside them is a dead bee; pollen still clinging to its legs.

That is something, to die doing the work that you were born to do...and to do it by defying the flight of expectation.

I, too, am fertile.

Chapter 1:

Two Paths, One Destination

The vision of a bear silhouetted in the darkness of my tent comes to me as I begin to explore what my work on ethics in ecopsychology is to become. I tell my colleague and friend, Betsy. Immediately she wants to talk about what the bear could mean: *Does this represent the project looming large? Why am I in a tent? After all, a tent is mobile and less likely to be thought of as a permanent presence.* My friend also pointed out that I saw only the outline of the head and the shoulders of the bear, which suggests academia.

Betsy and I go deeper into the metaphor and talk about the journey into ethical standards for ecopsychology as unchartered territory where—like the pioneers mapping the wilderness—this book is a way of telling others what I've seen so that they can find their way; the more people traveling the path, the greater the likelihood of the path being mapped. In this wilderness, the bear represents "the last true [symbol] of the primal, natural world," and how we, as co-inhabitants, respond to and protect their lands.[16]

The bear, like the missionary, will be the guide. This is a pilgrimage with two paths and one destination. One path considers how the interactions Christian missionaries had with indigenous populations might apply to our relationship with the rest of the natural world. The other path examines the lessons and insights that come from following the bear. In the end, our destination is to define, explore, and outline a code of conduct for both ecopsychology as the study of our relationship with our environment, and those of us who are interested in mindfully inhabiting the earth. In pursuit of that destination I discovered that bears are often associated with trees because, among other things, they climb them for a clear perspective.[16] With that in mind, the first tree to climb is that of the origins and history of ecopsychology.

ORIGINS AND HISTORY

The way that I view ecopsychology has evolved from the understanding that Theodore Roszak coined the term in his 1992 book, *The Voice of the Earth*.[18] Once I began connecting other people and areas of study to ideas that contributed to ecopsychology, I started thinking in terms of a family tree. When I sketched out the tree I focused on Roszak as the father until I realized Roszak considered Paul Shepard "the first ecopsychologist" because he was "the first thinker in the environmental movement to apply psychological categories to our treatment of the planet."[xii] Shepard was also referred to as an "environmental philosopher." Having a philosopher as the first ecopsychologist led me to the idea that the family tree was not a seed from an individual but from different fields of study.

In organizing my thoughts, I looked at the roots— or the origins—of the ecopsychology family tree as the fields of study that supported and fed it (Appendix E). The trunk of the tree is the entire field of psychology because Roszak was looking to "appeal to environmentalists and psychologists for a dialogue that would enrich both fields" rather than start an entirely new scientific field.[18] Because ecopsychology was nourished from other fields and focused on the application of our understanding of people, I considered it a branch of psychology rather than a trunk of its own tree. From the branch comes the twigs, or the most useful tool for identifying trees in the winter.[19] In this case, the twigs[xiii] are the eight guiding principles of ecopsychology that Roszak offered as a way to help focus the profession.[xiv] What I find interesting is that the tree, with these twig principles, ends just as it began at the root:

with ideas and concepts from multiple fields culminating into one interdisciplinary crown canopy.

THE PURPOSE

Since ecopsychology as the study of the human/nature relationship is meant, in part, to encourage a dialogue between environmentalists and psychologists, it is not surprising that ecopsychology also attempts to address communication problems with the general public.[18] In bringing together environmental issues with "the sphere of mind, soul, emotion" that is the study of psychology, ecopsychologists recognize that "there is an emotional bond between" us as humans and the natural environment from which we come.[18] Because of this, part of the story of ecopsychology is that we're not here to "conquer nature, but to flow, dance and balance with nature and each other, as do all other species."[21]

THE ROOTS

In considering "where psyche meets gaia," Roszak recognized that looking at the human animal as one with the natural world is not new, "but in fact its sources are old enough to be called aboriginal."[22] With ecopsychology drawing from ideas that have come before, the roots of the ecopsychological family tree, like the profession itself, "weaves science and psychiatry, poetry and politics together" to the point where the "priorities of the planet are coming to be expressed through our most private spiritual travail."[18] In following the lead of Roszak (as well as some others), I began looking at the roots of ecopsychology as including philosophy, cosmology, psychiatry, ecology, environmentalism, systems theory and transcendental. As this is a survey, I've chosen to skim the surface of only a few of those subjects here.

Philosophy

Philosophy began in the 1300s as the "love of knowledge [and] wisdom," and by 1771 it evolved into the "system a person forms for conduct of life."[23] Roszak considered philosophy to be the "faithful handmaiden of science, entrusted with keeping its master's methodological instruments [well-oiled] and polished."[18] What intrigues me about looking at ecopsychology as a family tree is the realization that those whose ideas helped to form the tree, are not necessarily considered ecopsychologists themselves. Quite often they are considered members of other fields of studies, and a few of them have a philosophical background. One example is Arne Naess who is considered to be a philosopher but is credited with coining the phrase *deep ecology movement* in 1972 while discussing "the ecology movement and its connections to values respecting nature and the inherent worth of other beings."[24] Another example is Paul Shepard, who has been labeled as the first ecopsychologist by Roszak and a "maverick 'human ecologist'" by ecophilosopher David Abram.[25]

Ecology

Ecology was coined in 1873 by zoologist Ernst Haeckel to define the study of a "dwelling place"[26] or the "relation of the animal both to its organic as well as its inorganic environment."[23] Roszak explains that "an ecological consciousness sees nature as alive, active, and capable of communicating with us."[22] Roszak also sees the goal of ecology as being a sustainable society where "each generation should meet its needs without jeopardizing the prospects for future generations to meet their own needs."

One point of reference by some contributors, including Roszak, is the Gaia hypothesis which was developed in 1972 to suggest that "all living things have a regulatory effect on the Earth's environment."[26] According to Roszak, "gaia...might be seen as the evolutionary heritage that bonds all living things genetically and behaviorally to the biosphere."[22]

Ecofeminism

By investigating gender roles,[18] the idea is that there are "human qualities that must be saved if the planet is to be healed."[27] I suggest that those qualities might include what Jane Goodall recognized as being helpful for women in research: patience, understanding "the needs and desires of nonverbal animals," and maintaining peaceful...[family] relationships."[28] According to psychotherapist Andy Fisher,[29] ecofeminists recognize that historically the "repressing and exploiting of women has gone hand-in-hand with the repressing and exploiting of the natural world."[xv]

Deep Ecology

Deep ecology is a type of environmentalism[30] that builds on a theme or preservationism[31] and appreciates diversity and the "value of all beings."[24] Naess was sympathetic to a rising global movement of ordinary people in response to "environmental degradation and other forms of violence against the natural world."[24] Deep Ecology scholar Warwick Fox proposed this field of study be called *transpersonal ecology* because it recognized people would care for the earth without being "morally persuaded" if they had a developed sense of the world that was both transpersonal and ecological. [25] The care of the earth, to me, indicates more of a relationship than any other part because there isn't just protection and reaction, there is involvement which suggests a back-and-forth connection.

Environmentalism

Environmentalism began in 1923 as a theory in the debate of nature versus nurture, and was used in the ecological sense beginning in 1972.[23] It's a movement to "improve and protect the quality of the natural environment" by recognizing that "other-than-humans, living things and the natural environment as a whole" deserve consideration in moral, political and social policies.[24] Despite the seemingly noble intentions, there is the sense that people are generally asked to sacrifice in order to "show more responsibility, more concern, better morals."[24] Ecopsychology, looking to move beyond "shocking and shaming the public,"[22] takes into account the impact people and the environment have on each other. In weaving the expanded perspective of life, or *ecology,* with the increasing understanding of how people respond and behave, or *psychology,* ecopsychology also goes beyond protection and reaction to include intentional involvement.

THE TRUNK

It seems to me that the trunk of the family tree is psychology because Roszak was looking to start a "new dialogue between scientific intellect and human need." The other reason psychology is the trunk of the tree is because "once upon a time all psychology was 'ecopsychology.'" Coining the term, according to Roszak, was meant to be a wakeup call and not a new field of study.[18] Should psychology embrace and return to a study that balances science and people with intellect and need, then the trunk of this tree could very well be labeled ecopsychology. Until such a time, Jungian analyst James Hillman agrees that "psychology, so dedicated to awakening human consciousness, needs to wake itself up to one of the most ancient human truths: we cannot be studied or cured apart from the planet."[32] Roszak saw poet William Blake as giving psychology his own kind of wakeup call when he noted concern that "science...screened the value of things, the beauty of things, the sacredness of things as if these qualities might not really be there."[33] In balancing science with humanity, psychology, I surmise, is not to simply conform itself to the scientific method but embrace all that *it is* and all that *it is not.* According to Roszak, Sigmund Freud admitted artists like Blake "had discovered the unconscious well before he had." This point, to me, recognizes that the wisdom of ecopsychology is in being an interdisciplinary field that incorporates all schools of thought so that no theory is arrived at in isolation or inherently missing part of the truth.

Psychology

Roszak defined psychology as "the study of human experience."[18] It evolved from being defined as the "study of the soul" in 1653 and the "study of the mind" in 1748, to its use in the "main modern behavioral sense" in 1895.[23] If a wakeup call is necessary as Roszak, Hillman, and Blake have indicated, then from this perspective I can see that a fuller understanding of experience must include the mind and soul as well as behavior.

Gestalt

Perception is the recognition of the voice of the earth in our bodies,[xvi] according to perceptual psychologist Laura Sewall.[34] Gestalt is the foundation of modern perception, and uses phenomenology to describe what one is experiencing directly, without limitations. It is a holistic theory that views the *whole* of anything as better than any *part*.[31] Another way to view this is that ecopsychologists recognize you cannot examine the human experience apart from the earth. Gestaltists, in fact, would look at the whole experience by including the relationships between the "organism and environment."[29]

Phenomenology

Phenomenologists describe the world "as it is actually lived" in order to show that human existence is essentially a network of evolving relationships.[29] Gestalt incorporated it as a way to humanize an otherwise sterile approach. The phenomenological tactic is not to "predict and control the world," but to "find those words that are true to our experience" and, like poetry, create a shift in that experience that brings "new awareness or understanding."

THE BRANCH

Ecopsychology, combining both ecology and psychology, can be seen as "psychologists in service to the Earth."[24] Roszak, in expanding on his original vision, noted that there have been several other names attributed to this growing field including psychoecology, ecotherapy, green therapy, reearthing, nature-based psychotherapy, and shamanic counseling to name a few.[xvii] Roszak[18] suggested that each name represents "one therapist's idea about how to include the more-than-human world in their work with clients."[xviii] While I am not a therapist, when I first began defining my practice I referred to it as narrative ecopsychology for its intentional use of story in enabling a connection with nature. Now that I've incorporated personal and professional coaching into my practice, I refer to my work as *wilderness coaching* because I have been inspired by the writings of Robert Greenway, Gary Ferguson, and Steven Harper, whose work has been referred to as a *wilderness practice* or *wilderness therapy*.[17] A wilderness practice is one that leaves behind the office for full immersion in a wild natural environment so that the focus turns to what emerges in the present moment.[xix] Mark Schroll, whom I consider the field historian, can trace the path of ecopsychology from conception with Fox and the deep ecology movement, to Greenway who called it psychoecology when Roszak attended discussion groups related to the topic in 1990.[36] This chapter is but a seed in the soil of the origins and history of ecopsychology because Schroll's work is so thorough, and to make the point that there is a freedom in building on the foundation rather than reconstructing it.

THE TWIGS

The eight guiding principles of ecopsychology include: getting in touch with our ecological unconscious in order to promote sanity; making real the idea that life and mind are a part of the universe that has and continues to evolve; healing the rift between the human animal and its natural environment; pulling from other disciplines ways of recovering the child-like wonder of the ecological ego; incorporating the spontaneously occurring sense of environmental responsibility that comes from identifying with our surroundings; addressing the need to conquer and dominate the environment; looking at limiting the impact industry has on the ecological ego; and recognizing that the needs and rights of the planet are of equal value as the needs and rights of the person.[xii] These guiding principles help to meet the goal of bridging the divide between the psychological and ecological by recognizing that the needs of the person and the planet are the same, and by weaving together ideas from the fields of ecology, cosmology, deep ecology, environmentalism, and ecofeminism.[18] The ecological ego, as a point of reference, is our core sense of reciprocity that matures from an open and affirming love of nature, to a sense of responsibility for the earth.[xx] It connects us to the rest of the evolving universe and can be suppressed or empowered based on our experiences.[xxi]

THE VIEW FROM HERE

Like a bear climbing a tree to get a better viewpoint, examining the origins and history of ecopsychology as a family tree can be seen as a way of finding our own perspective on the journey toward outlining a code of ethics for this area of study. The fact that the roots and crown canopy come together to form a whole tree, also illustrates how "no single philosophy can solve all of these problems" because "global progress requires broad cooperation."[24]

CHAPTER 2:

THE VALUE AND THE CHOICE

The idea of following the lead of the Christian missionary was born of an assignment in which I was asked to explore ethics and apply it to the field of ecopsychology. When I began, there was no direct or concise list of ethics for the field that I could find. In addition, there were a couple of books that gave me the idea of following the missionary: *Of Water and Spirit* by Malidoma Some´ and *The Other Side of Eden* by Hugh Brody. In *Of Water and Spirit* Christianity was viewed as contradictory when missionaries tried to 'tame' Some´ "to better fit in with society."[38] In *The Other Side of Eden* Brody was immersed in the native culture of Canada while trying to help assimilate the indigenous people into 'civilized' society. He was able to see the value of learning what the hunter-gatherers could teach him about "their own particular human genius...[and] human history."[39]

I was both awed and concerned by the picture Some´ and Brody painted. When the missionaries kept indigenous people from practicing their traditions, they lost their identity. In *Of Water and Spirit* the children could not speak their native language, and in *The Other Side of Eden* natives were not permitted to practice their skills. In the same way that language and skills can be lost without practice, we could lose our identity[39] without direct experience and continued connection with the rest of the natural world.[xxii]

On some level we seek connection even in the midst of our busy lives. I've talked to people who had never heard of ecopsychology and when I mentioned the importance of experiencing nature I could see and hear that the idea resonated with them. One person admitted that when she needed a break in the middle of the day she would look out her office window at a tree in a courtyard. Think about that in terms of how much time we used to be outside and how much time we now spend outside. I notice a difference in how I feel overall when I have a chance to immerse myself in nature and when I can't remember the last time I had that chance. As I point out in my blog posts _A Return to Life_[40] and _The Wilderness Makes Us Smarter,_ [41] just as Robert Greenway recognized it took his students three days to acclimate to their wilderness environment, research published in the May 2012 issue of Backpacker magazine shows that it takes three or four days of being immersed in the wilderness before we begin to experience a 50% increase in creative thought. That increase comes from a shift in the required constant focus and multi-tasking of our busy lives and the freedom to be present in the moment and follow a thought wherever it might lead. [41] Now consider all the ways we may limit our contact with the rest of nature. Some examples may include putting shoes on our feet, going indoors to sleep, and gathering in urban centers where the natural landscape is minimal, manicured, or not native to the area. If full immersion in the wilderness increases our creativity then it stands to reason that disconnection from the natural world, and the freedom to be present, reduces our creativity.

I thought Seattle was a wonderfully natural place until I read _Emerald City_ by environmental historian Matthew Klingle.[42] With that book I realized how manicured the city really is with its human-sculpted hillsides and foundation literally made of historical rubble. Seattle cannot return to its natural self because, just as people lose their native language and skills without practice, our environment can lose its own unique characteristics if its limits are exceeded, overwhelmed, or damaged.[xxiii] For example, European native forests were replaced by trees "designed to yield wood and pulp at a high rate indefinitely."[43] This caused the forests to lose their resiliency. What was the cost of change in this case? Changing an entire ecosystem to nonnative plants, to me, is like changing an entire culture to nonnative ideas[50] because it was the nonnative ideas of the missionaries that lead the native populations to lose the resiliency of their culture through a lack of practice.[39] What a code of ethics allows us to do is stop the quest to make things better before we've had the chance to "pay attention to the value of what's already there."[43]

THE BARRIER

I am reminded of the influence of colonialism on the indigenous people of the Barrier Island in my book, *Rooted in Water*.[44] Being isolated on the Sea Islands of the Southeastern coast of the United States have allowed slave descendants known as the Gullah Geechee to retain much of their African heritage. They were so removed from the mainland culture that they were left to their own devices and allowed to practice their traditions.[44] The Gullah Geechee are two groups of people. The Gullah retained more of their traditions because they were allowed to keep to themselves, while the Geechee spent more time with the European population and developed a 'bridge' language in order to communicate. The Barrier Islands protect the mainland just as they helped to protect the way of life for the Gullah Geechee. This means that if the Barrier Islands were to be submerged, damaged, or destroyed, then whatever hit them first—hurricane, pollution, etc.—would then have more of a direct route to the mainland.

Metaphorically, the Barrier Islands could represent indigenous culture and traditions. If they're wiped out, then next wave of assimilation could have a direct route to another segment of the population. As illustrated by the interconnectedness of ecopsychology as a field, genius is needed from different disciplines in order to solve the world's problems. To lose an entire culture means we have less wisdom to draw from when we turn to face the challenges that are to come. By allowing cultural diversity to thrive, we may find protection through knowledge and practices that demonstrate how to live in balance with the earth in different environments; if we ignore or diminish indigenous contributions, then we lose touch with our collective heritage and the invaluable knowledge that is ours to claim. It is one thing to understand that we are giving up our global cultural heritage and allow whole populations and species to disappear, it something else to let them disappear without so much as a thought as to what the implications might be. I believe to make an informed decision about how to conduct ourselves we must first discover the value of what might be lost.

THE MISSION

Before we continue to look at other ways to relate to the impact of Christian missionaries, let's begin with an initial point of reference. *Ethics*, by definition, are "rules of conduct" for behavior.[45] These rules can be applied to an individual, group, or profession. For our purpose, a *mission* is a group "sent by a church to carry on religious work" such as evangelizing in foreign lands or, in the case of Some,´ establishing schools, hospitals, etc. In looking at the origin of the word *mission,* I found that in the 1590s it meant 'sending.'[46] In the 1620s the act of 'sending' was done with the intent to engage in some kind of business. *Evangelization,* by comparison, is preaching the gospel and converting others to Christianity.[45] Metaphorically, ecopsychology can be seen as preaching about ecology and environmentalism while drawing upon the knowledgebase of psychology.

At the outset of my journey, I sought anything remotely related to 'Christian missionary ethics,' especially if it involved field work in a foreign land. I did this because, symbolically, going into foreign lands and going into unknown or wilderness territory were one in the same to me. For example, you may not know the customs and traditions of a given people upon arrival, so how you conduct yourself may put you in harmony or discord with the life around you. In a look at "the wilderness experience as a source of spiritual inspiration," Laura Fredrickson and Dorothy Anderson defined wilderness as "a region which contains no permanent inhabitants [and] no possibility for motorized travel."[47] According to the Wilderness Act, it's "an area where the earth and its community of life are untrammeled by man, where man himself is a visitor who does not remain."[48] Wilderness, in this case, would be a natural area untouched by industry and unspoiled by humankind.

By bringing in the Christian missionary as a guiding metaphor, I wanted to know if there was a way of honoring native people and their traditions without taking advantage of or alienating them. I have a friend who participates in a lot of group work. In our conversations, she has pointed out that there seems to be more resistance when new people become part of a group already wanting to make changes without first learning about the group's history, methodology, or traditions. When considering what Christian missionary work could teach us about living in balance with the rest of life, we can view explaining ecopsychology, or our way of relating to the rest of the earth, as evangelizing. Establishing a code of conduct for ecopsychology can then be a way of ensuring that we are careful to identify where the boundaries should be so that our message is received and the value of the information, whether accepted or rejected, is more fully considered.

THE VALUE OF INDIGENOUS INFORMATION

Just as the wilderness is free from the influence of industry or humankind, according to the field of indigenous psychology,[50] truly indigenous populations are themselves native to a place and without external influence. Indigenous, by definition, has been defined as "born from within."[49]

The Rite to Know

The original assignment for this book challenged me to apply a code of ethics to the field of ecopsychology, so I focused on the work that I wanted to do. At the time I had an interest in wilderness therapy and was looking at becoming a wilderness quest guide. *A wilderness quest* is a ritual based on a Native American rite of passage. In a quest people sever ties with their old lives and selves, cross a threshold into the wilderness where they fast for a vision before being incorporated back into their community.

Gary Ferguson, a nature writer that followed at-risk youth in a wilderness program for two seasons,[51] described the wilderness quest process as having four intentions: "letting go of an old way of being...the acknowledgment or acceptance of a wandering time...the glimpsing of a new self; and...the rooting of a new way of being." Ferguson illustrated these intentions with the Iroquois story of Nekumonta. In the story many of Nekumonta's people became ill. He went into the "dark heart of the forest" to find healing herbs for his people. Nekumonta searched for three days and nights, asking the animals he encountered for help. After the "darkest part of the night," when pleadings to the Creator were answered, Nekumonta awoke, searched, and found the healing waters, which he took back to the village." From that point on he was known as Chief of the Healing Waters.[xxiv]

If we view Nekumonta as an ecopsychologist in search of healing for his people, and the quest as a framework for our code of ethics, then the code must first serve to free us from our old ways of thinking, and the associations that may hold us back or keep us from moving forward. We must intentionally cross the threshold into areas where we can ask for assistance from the rest of the natural world and hear the response. Finally there must be something tangible that we bring back to our community to share.

A quest is a death-rebirth initiation ritual that has both informed cultures throughout history and removed the person from the noise of urban life where "the voice of nature itself" speaks.[52] Modern day quest programs such as the School of Lost Borders[53] and Soulcraft[54] see the indigenous practice as a leveraging of "the dangerous, bold, risk-taking energies of youth" in a way that informs and sustain the community because, like Nekumonta, they return with a unique gift they can share.[xxv]

From Another's Eyes

In our travel to a foreign land or into the wilderness, we have an opportunity to become aware of the assumptions we hold or the rituals we practice without thinking. I first traveled to Australia in November 2007 and quickly realized Thanksgiving traditions, eating without utensils, and many of the television shows I reference to communicate were no longer part of a shared experience. As a result, I am now a proponent of traveling outside of one's home town, country, or comfort zone. According to Stephen Bochner in his study of culture shock, "we really only become aware of the presence of a behavioural imperative when it is infringed or disregarded."[56] Nan Sussman saw travel as a way to "increase intercultural sensitivity, provide alternative ways to behave and interpret the world, [as well as] improve understanding of why people in other countries behave and think the way they do."[57] If how we identify ourselves culturally is something we don't consciously think about, then "most adults are not aware of how their thinking and acting and interpreting has been shaped."[57] While foreign travel can raise our awareness, a code of ethics can also serve as a tool to make us aware of the assumptions we carry.

Knowledge and Growth

The value of indigenous information comes from both human and other-than-human populations. According to Ted Andrews, who teaches in the metaphysical and spiritual fields,[61] the bear relates to the initial stages of things, so it's not surprising that as I began to revisit my work on ethics, a bear appeared to me. Bear is also often associated with trees because they'll scratch their backs on them, mark them up as signposts, as well as climb them to change their perspective. *Bear* and *Tree*, according to Andrews, represent knowledge and things that grow.[61] What I find particularly telling in the context of this ethical exploration is that Bear asks questions that are relevant to this ethical exploration:

- Is my judgment off?
- How about those around me?
- Am I recognizing what is beneficial in my life?
- Am I seeing the core of good, deep within all situations?
- Am I being too critical of myself or others?

These questions are relevant because they can, like a code of conduct, serve as a reminder to stop and question our basic assumptions about a situation. To illustrate, if I decide that I am in fact recognizing what is beneficial in my life, stopping to consider the question will make me aware of that fact. If I decide I am not recognizing what is beneficial in my life then the question will not only make me aware, it provides me with the opportunity to change the situation.

SIGNPOSTS

While the bear leaves signposts on trees to mark a path, at this stage of our journey I have found the following markings worth considering:

- **Identify what is being evangelized.** What message am I delivering? What points am I trying to make?
- **Identify if the goal is to convert.** For transformation to be sustained, a person cannot

feel pushed into it. How important is it for me that change be the result of me interaction?

- **Know the value of change**. Determine what, if anything, is already being done in a given situation. If nothing is being done, what has been tried? By determining the value of what is in place I'll have a better idea what the cost of change will be.

- **Change perspective.** How can I shift to a view of the forest if all I've been focused on is a single tree? At the same time, if the relationship of the forest is all that I've seen how can I make sure not to lose sight of a single tree? Do I need to go to another location in order to see myself and my mission clearly?

- **Practice in order to maintain**. If I don't practice my traditions, they can be lost. By the same token, if I don't share my traditions with the young, they will not be in place generations to come.

- **Consider what interactions reveal.** Does my relationship with the immediate environment reflect my relationship with the rest of the natural world? If I don't care for animals, am I really committed to caring for myself?

- **Account for the need to change**. Have I identified a problem and the need to change? Am I ready to move forward so that change is sustainable? How does the metaphor of the bear or the missionary apply to my individual journey?

These signposts are intended to help each of us become more aware of our impact and what we're trying to accomplish with our mission. These markings are also a way to provide guidelines for how to explain the value of our work to the rest of our community.

Divine Form

I set aside this day for writing, not simply the act of writing for its own sake, but delving into books and following wherever curiosity might lead.

When I begin my day I like getting settled by asking for guidance from the world around me. The answers I receive set the scene for the journey on which I am to embark.

Today I am uncertain if I should seek guidance for the day or... Before I can say 'week' I nearly walk into a black ball dangling before me at eye level.

It is a spider.

There is no doubt as to who my guide is in this moment. This little ball of being dangling before me at eye level is positioned from the ceiling the perfect distance for basking in the morning sun.

Wisdom is here.

The Spider tells me that today is a lesson in balance between the past and future, physical and spiritual, male and female.

Spider reminds me that this journey is about looking at time as an expanse that connects generation to generation, that which has occurred and is to occur, balancing change with direction.[63]

CHAPTER 3:

TRANSFORMATION AND INSIGHT

"Walk with me and I will show you the river," says Brother Raccoon to Busy Mouse who asks about a strange sound he had roaring in his ears. So begins the story of the Sacred River[62] as told to and published by Steven Foster and Meredith Little. *The Roaring of the Sacred River*, like the story of Nekumonta, is a metaphor for the ritual of the wilderness quest. Raccoon[63] is a relative of Bear,[xxvi] so as Brother Raccoon is a guide in the journey to the Sacred River, Bear is our guide in the journey to an ethical standard. Both take us on "strange paths" until we reach our destination. Along the way we find that the Sacred River, not unlike ethics, is "deep and clear in places, and murky in others" and "it is powerful" as our experiences with it can make us aware of our basic assumptions, direct us how to move forward, and identify consequences when we choose not to honor it.

STRANGE PATHS

In the story of the *Sacred River* Busy Mouse sees his reflection in the water, and is asked to jump as high as he can to change his perspective. He does, and is able to see the Sacred Mountain before falling to Earth and into the river. Despite his fear from having fallen into the Sacred River, Busy Mouse (renamed Jumping Mouse because of his accomplishment) goes back to tell others. The others are unsure of what Jumping Mouse tells them because he's wet and he can't explain why. Still, hearing the roaring of the Sacred River in his ears, Jumping Mouse decides to go out in search of the Sacred Mountain.

As this story applies to our journey, we've heard the call to have an ethical standard for ourselves or ecopsychology. Bear has offered to show us the way much like Brother Raccoon offered to walk with Busy Mouse to the Sacred River. When Busy Mouse came to the river, he looked into it and saw his reflection. If the river is a metaphor for a code of ethics, then examining the code should enable us to recognize and appreciate our work and stories. Through this reflection the code transforms from mere words to understanding. Professionally, a code of conduct helps us to explain the value of our work to the community. As we continue to pursue the Sacred Mountain of vision that relates to our career goals or our profession, we remain focused by the roar of the Sacred River (code of ethics).

WHERE THE BEAR LEADS

Not only are bears related to raccoons, they're also connected to the Greek Goddess Artemis, who is known for being—among other things—the Goddess of the Wilds, Wilderness, and Wildlife.[64] Several animals are considered sacred to Artemis,[xxvii] but the bear was so important—as an animal as well as the constellation Ursa Major—that if you were to harm one, you'd likely encounter the wrath of Artemis.[xxviii] A virgin who held purity in high regard, Artemis was celebrated in a rite of passage where girls between the age of five and fifteen would dress in robes and act as bears before they would be given away in marriage. Artemis was not only known for being a "fierce protector of young," but a protector of the pure to the point where she killed Callisto, in bear form, for failing to preserve her virginity.[64]

THE MYTHIC MESSAGE

While it may seem odd to consider the divine form of a bear with Christian missionaries, I am reminded that myths "deal with great human problems" and give us an idea of "how to live a human lifetime under any circumstance."[65] In this case, Artemis is a metaphor, a guiding story for the ethics involved in ecopsychology, and how to conduct ourselves in the wilds. Myths suggest that we can continue to look inward while examining the stories of other cultures, and learning to consider another way of life[66] so that we never have to wake up forgetting that there are other possibilities.[67] While we can continue to meet with people who are like us, we can be reminded through others' stories that "there are people in the world who understand where [our] tears are coming from."[68] Likewise, we can "touch a chord in the person listening" by sharing our own stories. [68] When we combine rites of passage with "wilderness solitude and the ecological messages conveyed by myth," we're helping with the process of maturing the whole person[69] by waking them up to compassion, which is the "the beginning of humanity." In these moments God, like the one in you, are born.[66]

A Sacred Connection

Artemis earned her title of Goddess of the Wilds or Goddess of the Wilderness, from her preference for "being out in the wilds."[64] An example of the wilds would include Yellowstone National Park, which, in 1872 was the first ever wilderness area permanently set aside to be preserved. In 1885, the Adirondack Forest Preserve was established in New York State as "a region to be kept forever in its wilderness condition." In 1890 Yosemite National Park was established in California, as were voluntary associations such as The Sierra Club (1892) and The Wilderness Society (1924). These groups were set up to "create a more intimate relationship between the human community and the wild world about us."[70] These territories and organizations illustrate the principle that what is important enough to keep, like wilderness and our ability to immerse ourselves in it, should be preserved and shared so that others may know of it. Wilderness, you may recall, is nature untouched by industry or unspoiled by people. If those that came before us had not preserved territory or created those organizations, would we have had the chance to know what true wilderness was or even the chance to see how it differs from the environment in which we spend our daily lives?

Even as we may unknowingly embody Artemis, we are "spiritually affected by the beauty and majesty of the wilderness, to feel a sacred connection to the elements and the great mystery of being part of the universe."[65] When I quested for a life vision I did so with the intent of letting go of a relationship that had deeply wounded me. My partner was unfaithful and emotionally abusive and I had not forgiven myself. I returned to the solo site where I fasted, performed a ritual of pouring out water to let go of the pain, and hugged myself to gather to me the parts of my soul that were lost. When I was done I saw that the tree limb that marked my territory was glowing. I silently asked if I could take it back with me. Feeling as though I had permission, I bent over and lifted the branch. Immediately I both heard music floating in the breeze and saw the bright color of a butterfly dancing on that same whisper of wind. My insides leapt with excitement as I felt acknowledged and blessed by the universe. I no longer feel the burden of guilt that used to make me visibly cringe. Instead I focus on being a light in a dark place by combining my understanding of ecopsychology and my skills as a life coach into a practice that allows me to work with other wounded hearts.

The beauty of nature can be a trigger for having a mystical experience, which is "the sense of unity, the experience of timelessness and spacelessness, the sense of union with humankind, the universe, and God as well as feelings of positive affect, peace, joy, and love." These experiences can lead to psychospiritual changes in our thoughts, emotions, attitudes, core beliefs and behaviors, which is revealed as a change in our priorities more so than a change in our character.[71] This is illustrated in what happened to Paul on the road to Damascus. Paul, who was said to have a "mystical bent," has also been described as fanatic in his persecution of Christians.[71] On his way to continue the persecution, he was "knocked to the ground and struck blind by a light."[71] That moment did not change the passion with which Paul worked, it changed where he directed it as he went on to establish and mentor a number of Christian churches. Additionally, many prophets were "inspired by nature or withdrew into it to tap its wisdom." I find it intriguing that immersion in nature can lead to a spiritual experience and the word *religion* comes from 're-ligio' or 'reconnecting.' This demonstrates our desire to connect "with something larger than the human race and our own creations."[72] While I view sharing the message of ecopsychology as evangelizing, I'm not saying it is specifically a religion. It seems to me that that religion and the natural world experience are interconnected, and the practice of the prophets illustrates a good point for ecopsychology: connection is not a one-time occurrence, but a sustained practice if it is to continue. If we do not tend to our relationship with the divine or the natural world, or reconnect when we've become disconnected, then we will ultimately lose that relationship as well as that part of our identity.

Where the Missionary Leads

Following the missionary as a way of identifying the ethics of working with indigenous populations can provide us with a model of how we can or should interact with the rest of the natural world. For this part of the journey I've included academic literature addressing ethics and the Christian missionary, focusing on the natural world, humanity of indigenous people, its application to a profession, and the Eur-Asian perspective so that we can examine our own perceptions.

Judging Others

In looking at the *History, Ethics, and the Purposes of Comparison,*[74] I realized that "one compares things of the same sort in order to judge" which is better than the other. This suggests that a missionary would judge a current belief system against their own. This could be problematic if missionaries determine their belief system to be superior to that of another culture or people. If a missionary—or an ecopsychologist doing field work—recognizes that comparisons are for his or her own purposes and not necessarily for "the sake of pure knowledge," then he or she can be mindful of comparisons being made, and account for possible prejudice in his or her work or interactions.

In thinking about evangelizing ecopsychology, I wonder if it is enough to simply tell others the 'good news' of a sustainable relationship with the rest of the natural world. I think about conversations around global warming and climate change and I remember that the discussion has gone back and forth as to whether or not the scientific data is accurate or was manufactured to service one agenda or another. In the end the sharing of scientific data about the effects of human behavior on changing our climate[75] did not lead the United States, for example, to sign the Kyoto Protocol.[xxix]

What makes the situation of missionaries challenging is measuring success. Success, in their case, means converting someone to Christianity. If we are clear about the boundaries between the belief system we represent, and the practices of the person or culture with whom we are interacting, then we can better share our ideas while respecting the traditions of others. Similarly, when we go out on a trail into our local parks or nearby wilderness, we are entering a pre-existing way of being for the animals and plants that already inhabit those places. If we don't account for our actions or judgments, they could lead to "ignorance, incomprehension, misperception...misinformation," or, in its more subtle form, misconception and a loss of objectivity.

NATURE ETHICS

Grace G. Campbell reviewed *Nature Ethics by Marti Kheel*.[76] Though this is a book review, Campbell's insights offer another perspective about the natural world. Most notably, as we look to balance the male and the female (or the dominant and the nurturing) ways of being, Campbell recognizes the fact that environmental ethics are masculine in nature, and Kheel's work "lays the groundwork for a new ecofeminist framework" that is inclusive and compassionate as well as ecological in its sense of values." This can serve as a reminder for myself and others that it is easier to be in balance when nature is not perceived as an entity that needs to be controlled, or when we don't allow our unease to lead us to "the cutting down of forests, [and] the annihilation of native people."[66]

Campbell highlights the contrast of dominance/submission that comes into view when looking at the use of the language with regards to ethics and judgment. For example, I was introduced to the landmark in the red center of Australia by its aboriginal name—Uluru—rather than its European name—Ayers Rock. Those two names represent two different cultures, stories, and ways of knowing and experiencing the land.

Moreover, I call the large volcanic landmass that is visible from Lake Washington, Mount Rainier. I was surprised to learn that it had its own indigenous name: Talal, Tahoma, or Tacoma. This information added a layer of meaning I would have otherwise missed. Campbell notes that Kheel consciously chooses "to use other-than-human animals to remind [us] that humans are also animals and to stress kinship ties" so that we can get at the reasons why we may take a superior or dominating approach to our relationship with the rest of nature.[76]

MISSION AND HUMAN IDENTITY

What captivated me about *Mission and Human Identity* is the reference to identity and the point that "Jesus Christ is the key to human reconciliation" in Christianity. At the time, those that were not reconciled were considered not fully human.[78] This puts the missionary in the position of judging another as needing to be reconciled, and if they were not, as being less than human or not equal. A code of ethics that respects all life would mean those people who were not reconciled would still be revered. I realize now that it's not just important that we protect the needs and rights of plants and animals, it is important that all life be valued so that, for example, even people who are labeled *animal* can be recognized as having rights.

If missionary work is not just about proclaiming Christianity, but about cooperating with "neighbors of other faiths for common purposes in society"[78] then all life has value because everyone contributes to the common good. If we consider the identity of the words used as well, reconciliation is normally translated as "*katallagē,* or *exchange.* If all life has value then, in this instance, Christianity is about coming to Christ to exchange sin for salvation and not our identity for deliverance.[78]

ETHICS AND THE ENGINEER

Ethics and the Engineer[79] offers us a look at the ethics of theology in making engineering a practice of well-being which I believe can illustrate how a code of ethics for the study of ecopsychology can be applied to both the profession as well as practice of mindful living as a co-inhabitant of earth. By combining ethics in a profession with a theological approach, W. R. Bowen points out that the commandments to love God and neighbor (Appendix F) combine intention and values, with understanding responsibility as being "'accountable *for* and accountable *to,*' and nurturing 'a positive sense of vocation or calling.'"[79] For Bowen this meant "more attention should be given to responsible creativity" by the engineer so that the priority is "serving life and society.'"[78] As ecopsychology intends to keep the voice of the earth an intentional part of the conversation, a code of ethics would then serve as a reminder that each ecopsychologist and co-inhabitant is accountable *for* and *to* the earth in their practice on a local and global scale.

When Bowen proposes that the focus needs to be on "technical ingenuity" instead of on "helping people," I am reminded that Theodore Roszak called for ecopsychology to be "postindustrial not anti-industrial" so that we can question our urban-industrial culture without rejecting the "technological genius of our species or some life-enhancing measure of the industrial power we have assembled."[80] Bowen went on to bring in the language of "I" which recognizes that "the world of 'I' and 'IT' is that of experiencing and using."[79] *I use IT to achieve my goals.* 'I' and 'YOU,' on the other hand, sees the "uniqueness and integrity of the person...but acknowledges that the interaction may be brief and lacking in intimacy." *I work with YOU to achieve our goals.* The 'I' and 'THOU' relationship might come across as a "primitive message of the New Testament," but it is in that formality that we may find we're equals. *I and THOU achieve goals.* Bowen views this as divine personhood, which is the highest honor you can bestow on another. Divine personhood, represented as *I-THOU*, gives us both a way to see each other as an equal and a way to remember to put the other first. If a code of ethics for ecopsychology is about valuing all life, one way we can remind ourselves of this intention is to adjust our language. We are not to *use* nature to achieve our goals, therefore nature is not an *it*. We can be in service to each other so that *thou* are *with* me. By referring to nature as *thou*, we recognize that we are engaged in a partnership.

PROTESTANT ETHICS

Lauren Pfister examines Christian attitudes from a EurAsian perspective in *Protestant Ethics Among Chinese Missionaries*. During the timeframe referenced by this work, Western culture and Christianity were associated with colonial aggression, also referred to as "religious colonization."[82] Pfister noted that being accommodating and appreciating indigenous culture was an "unusual approach to Christian mission work," which led to rejection of the "Lutheran form of orthopraxy and [adoption of] something more sectarian."[82]

My intent with looking at the work of the missionary was, in part, to see if there were any interactions with indigenous populations that were consensual. I also wanted to see what lessons could be applied to interactions with the rest of the natural world. I not only find, from Pfister's work, that a consensual interaction is rare, it seems that when Christianity is a choice and not a command, the perspective of the missionary changes. In fact, with an "indirect" and "less confrontational form of missionary education" religion classes were not required despite being offered, converts were not baptized, and Christian literature was provided for students" as an option and not a requirement. In the end success was not measured by conversion but by "the greatness of the tasks one achieves rather than the words one speaks."[82] It would then seem that if we enter into a consensual interaction with the wilderness we might also come away with a change in perspective if not a change in our definition of success.

SCOTTISH MISSIONARIES

Scottish Missionaries and African Healers provides a revealing look at thought, language, and the 'colonial situation' from the perspective of the Christian medical missionary. [83] In this situation there appears to not only be a need to convert, but a need to demonstrate the "the superiority of Western medicine" so that the missionaries could maintain public support at a time when one quarter of them were dying from illness.[83] The missionaries would refer to the African healers as "priest-physicians" and claim that indigenous medicine was "based on superstition, ignorance, false religious beliefs and lack of scientific knowledge," while also suggesting that "'native' medicine could be a source of new, effective drugs."[83]

I am reminded of the *I-IT* relationship in finding the usefulness of the drug without the knowledge of administering it. Few attempts were made to understand the African culture because the assumptions were that it was inherently flawed with the 'native doctors' wielding "considerable power" by "playing on the fears and supernatural beliefs of their patients."[62] While an *I-THOU* view of the relationship would have put the African healers on more equal footing and allowed the medical missionaries to acknowledge that some of the healers had, in fact, properly diagnosed severe illness.

What concerns me the most is that this misinformation campaign was carried out in order to preserve the mission. If you are the only people to interact with an indigenous population and share your impressions of them, that may be all the information the rest of the world may ever get about that population until and unless others go and investigate for themselves. During this time publications paid more attention to stories about the "medical missionary armed with the light of the Gospel and medical science." Even the use of terms such as 'witch-doctor' demonized native culture and glorified a "medical mission triumphing over the African doctors" that practiced witchcraft. Because these views also reflected that of British culture at that time, a code of ethics should include a provision that accounts for the cultural context of the mission and the missionary.

Ethical Issues and Guidelines

Craving a more concise list of ethical standards, I turned to *Ethical Issues and Guidelines in Psychology.* In this book Philip Banyard and Cara Flanagan explained that *ethics* is a framework for judging right from wrong for a select group of people while *morals* are a more socially agreed upon set of guidelines for behavior.[84] In adopting part of the ethical framework discussed by Banyard and Flanagan, I can see the need for ecopsychology to include a debriefing process in order to determine the impact of an exercise on a participant as well as the need for follow up such as counseling or restoration.

As I continued to pull from Bayard and Flanagan I discovered that the ethical issues of consent, harm and privacy all have to do with the rights of the participant, which could include an entire community in terms of socially sensitive research that may bring about implications or consequences. In such cases the community could participate in the research process or review the final report.

Ethical guidelines for ecopsychologists can also be seen as important in helping to check on the wellbeing of the system in place which can include the system of psychology and the realization that therapy is also a business with bills to pay.[xxx] Part of checking the wellbeing of the system can be examining whether we are collectively "turning as many of us as possible into 'victims' prepared to pay for therapy," or whether the study of human experience continues to ignore the rest of the planet.

In the end, these considerations were what I was hoping to find in the context of a missionary/convert relationship. Cultural sensitivity can be a way to embrace differences and help us communicate so that others "understand, believe, regard as relevant to themselves and are likely to act upon."[84] The goal then becomes honoring the world of the participant without forcing what we want on them or trying to change them because we want to get rid of them. [84]

CHAPTER 4:

FRESH EYES

After seeing where both the bear and the Christian missionary could take us in terms of ethical standards for ecopsychology, let's follow some foundational texts to see what other insights emerge. For me, nearly two years removed from the original paper that started this journey, I intend to approach these works with fresh eyes, or at least a new perspective.

RESTORING THE EARTH

In *Ecopsychology*,[86] the anthology that was edited by Theodore Roszak, Mary E. Gomes, and Allen D. Kanner, my new focus on ethics led me to the 'ecological equivalent' of the *Golden Rule*: "each generation should meet its needs without jeopardizing the prospects for future generations to meet their own needs." This suggests that we must live sustainably so that there is something to *tell* the next generation, as well as *show* them. Isn't this a sacrificial attitude most, if not all parents take? If that is the case then it seems to me that we are all parents to the generations to come, whether we shoulder that responsibility or not.

How do we do this? In the chapter *Are We Happy Yet?* Alan Thein Durning points out that the first thing we have to do is "inform consumers of the damage they are causing and how they can avoid it." Like coaching, training, or any form of transporting people from the state of 'not knowing' to 'knowing,' you have to be clear about *what* is needed, not just *that* it is needed. To some extent consumers have been informed and are changing their behavior which, according to Durning, is evidenced by the fact that when purchasing a car most people will now consider the environmental impact instead of just their personal reputation.

Durning also makes the point that in order to live sustainably we must move at the pace of a "sunset stroll by the water's edge."[xxxi] This reminds me of when I was shadowing a crew for Odyssey Wilderness Programs, which focuses on helping families with 'at-risk youth.' We were on their vessel, the Resolution, and there was so little wind in the beginning of our journey that we had to row quite a bit. At one point, as the sun beat down and the majesty of Mount Baker towered over us from the horizon, one of the teens on the boat asked if this was an area with a large sea lion population. The captain told him no, that we were just going slow enough to notice all their heads popping up out of the water.

A sustainable pace, in this case, is one that is slow enough to notice and take in what is happening around us. Part of an environmental ethic is not just adopting a sustainable pace, but also changing the way we see our relationship with the rest of the natural world; recognizing that, as Laura Sewell puts it, "we are within the biosphere" instead of "on a planet."[86] Slowing down and immersing ourselves in silence can be viewed as an example of what can be done to remind and allow us to listen to what nature is telling us.

LET IT DO YOU

My own slowing down occurred when I traveled to Uluru as a refuge from my life by immersing myself in the culture and place. My life-changing experience began when the guide told me not to be a typical tourist and *do* Uluru, but to spend a moment to stop and take it all in. In essence, he said, "don't do Uluru, let it do you." I was mindful of his words when I would stop and let the summer breeze caress my face. By the time the three-day tour was over, I had forgotten the personal angst that had initiated the trip.

During that journey I had been isolated from everyone I knew, touched by the stories of the aboriginals, and surrounded by the landscape that inspired those stories. I had come to realize that "wilderness journeys, nature walks, and adventure sports, when sensitively undertaken, can catalyze an intense bonding with the Earth as a nurturing parent."[86] Because I intentionally participated in the experience of Uluru, I felt connected with the culture and environment. I still do four years later. What the study of ecopsychology does is recognize the power of an experience such as the one in Uluru, and rather than stripping away that power, encourages a practice that maintains the connection with the earth. As we learn to maintain it, we can then serve as advisers to the people who are to come so that they never have to know a disconnected life.[xxxii]

CHANGING THE WORLD

While writing this book I came across the African proverb: "educate a boy, and you educate an individual. Educate a girl, and you educate a community."[89] An example of this is my mother. In an age of distributed rather than extended families, it is my mother, not my father, who began sharing the names and birthdates of relatives. When I revisited the book, *Cultural Creatives,* I noticed that under the section *Importance of Women* was a reminder that a valid way of understanding something involves "sympathy for others...taking the viewpoint of the one who speaks, seeing personal experiences and first-person stories as important ways of learning, and embracing an ethic of caring."[89] It was my mother who finally realized that my brother and I have not had many opportunities to truly sit with our relatives. If we had, we might have already heard the random but meaningful tales that make up our family history. And while, for some indescribable reason, my mother suddenly began sending emails documenting our lineage, I'm sure that there are still quite of few stories that have never met our ears. This is an example of a disconnection in my own personal history, but it can also illustrate the global importance of sharing our stories and having direct contact with one another as a way of connecting, building relationships, and passing along information.

In the chapter *Becoming a Cultural Creative*, Paul H. Ray and Sherry Ruth Anderson tell the story of futurist Willis Harman. Harman attended a workshop meant to be a "nonreligious discussion of ethics and life principles" hosted by a Stanford law professor. The experience turned out to be a retreat involving "extended meditations and soft classical music in the background." Harman felt 'tricked' because he would not have attended the event if he had known what would really happen. As a result of the experience, and in spite of his reaction, Harman evolved from working as an engineer to working as a researcher and futurist.[89]

The striking aspect of Harman's experience is the deception involved, which begs the question: is it ethical for a workshop to outline one agenda or experience and deliver another? In reviewing what I've discovered about ethical standards to this point, I appreciate the need to explain what and why the experience would or could change. I also appreciate the need to give the attendees a chance to express their reactions to the change in agenda. A debriefing should happen regardless, but something to address the difference in the workshop content and to determine if some other kind of follow up is needed also seems appropriate.

Although there is generally a certain level of commitment of time and travel for retreats, it should still be noted that if people do not wish to participate— especially after learning what the agenda or experience is really about—they should be given the chance to join in, opt out, and/or be reimbursed. What we are not privy to in this story is why the content was marketed as something different than it was, and what was done to acknowledge and address the reaction of those in attendance.

Upon observing the difference between ethics and morals I found it interesting that since the 1960s Americans have taken on more complex moral causes such as the well-being and fair treatment of women, children, people of color, preserving the earth, the sacredness of nature, inner psychological and spiritual experience, and personal responsibility.[89] The reason for this, according to Ray and Anderson, is that this is the generation that 'woke up' and asked new moral questions that have garnered new moral answers. Asian spiritual teachers even noticed that their Western students initially weren't interested in the "essentials of ethics" and were more likely to burn "their bridges with the past." A generation later, in the 1980s and 1990s, the focus shifted to "social and planetary good."[89] In retrospect, this evolution in causes leads me to wonder if once certain needs are met, we are free to expand our concerns to other areas of life.[91] In his look at

what motivates people, Abraham Maslow theorized that
once a person's needs for survival were met he or she were
free—or more inclined—to strive for higher needs such as
love, esteem, and self-acutalization.[91] In other words, as we
fulfill our basic needs, our focus can shift to larger needs
like environmental issues and spiritual experiences.

With regards to care and preservation of our
environment more specifically, Ray and Anderson noted
that it was in 1999 when Reverend Sally Bingham began to
connect the concern for "global climate change
and...collective responsibility" to the church.[89] This has led
us to move from individual concerns to a focus on values
and worldview.[91] Susan Clayton and Gene Myers, whose
work I will explore later, noted the grounding of
"stewardship ethics" in the Bible as a contributing factor in
environmental virtue taking hold in the United States.[92]
From this, our moral virtues and duties are shaped.

PSYCHOLOGY IN THE SERVICE OF LIFE

To Andy Fisher, ecopsychology is an attempt to
reverse our domination of nature psychologically. For him,
the goal is to "grant the natural world its own subjectivity,
agency, or personhood" so that we see the rest of the
natural world as our equal and protest whatever stops that
from happening.[93] Considering that "not everyone feels
compelled to defend a mountain," I am mindful of the need
to decide for oneself if the mountain matters at all, and if
so, determining how much it does matter. If I decide that
the mountain matters, I must "reconcile the conflicting
tasks of being faithful to [my] subject and maintaining [my]
credibility." This balance of faith with credibility should
not come at the expense of growing awareness. That is to
say that the mountain may not matter to me at this point in
my current level of awareness, but that doesn't mean it

will never matter to me because what I know and understand today may not be what I know and understand tomorrow.

CONSERVATION PSYCHOLOGY

Conservation Psychology was something I referenced while looking at how our experience in nature could inspire us to better care for the rest of the natural world. Since "people with a future orientation were more likely to engage in environmentally protective behaviors,"[92] it seems to me that an ethical code of conduct for ecopsychologists would intentionally account for the future. Referencing future generations can be a way for us to think beyond our lifetime, acknowledge what we've inherited, and recognize what we're passing along.

In searching for what the code of ethics would be for conservation psychology and ecopsychology as professions, I discovered that they were listed as an 'interest area' on the American Psychological Association website. While this led me to wonder if the APA code of ethics would suffice in studying ecopsychology (See Chapter 5), I also reached out to the Conservation Psychology office and was told that the closest thing to a code of ethics at the moment was the moral ethics section of the *Conservation Psychology* text. What stood out to me in the text was the notion that if we're to meet the environmental challenges of our time, then we must work together despite our differences in values, views, and circumstances. This would ensure that "our attention shifts from individual morality to our collective ability to recognize, reflect upon, and reasonably address the value questions we face."[92]

OUT OF THE SHADOW

Rinda West, in *Out of the Shadow*, asks "who speaks for the land?"[94] She suggests that environmental ethics, ecopsychology, and ecocritism are the fields challenging us to go beyond the human perspective when it comes to ethics. This revolves around the awareness that we view nature as more than an *it* from which we benefit, but a *thou* that has equal rights to exist. The works of African and American Indian writers support West's supplication to approach people and our place in nature from a different perspective; these works deepen our understanding and help us to care more for what is not *us* or *just like us.*[94] By looking through another's eyes, we may be able to see ourselves more clearly, and that deeper understanding can be considered part of the value of indigenous wisdom.

NATURE AND THE HUMAN SOUL

Bill Plotkin notes that for a child to become a full-fledged member of a family, she must model "a coherent and consistent set of values, a system of ethics and principles for making choices." In order for a child to model behavior, she must first have it modeled for her.[95] How do you model your relationship with nature for others? If you're not sure, consider the behavior of the young people in your life. Are their behaviors a reflection of what you've told them or a reflection of what you've shown them? When I hiked around Uluru, my guide informed me that I had the option of climbing to the top. While I had the option, the aboriginals had requested that I, and anyone with access, refrain because the ground was sacred to them. Despite expressing a deep desire to see the view from the top, my guide expressed a deeper respect for the wishes of the indigenous people of the area.

At the time I realized I was a child when it came to my awareness of the importance of our relationship with the rest of the natural world. My guide had modeled for me an understanding of the landscape and its people, as well as a way to place respect for the natural world ahead of my own desires.

How we identify with nature can be shaped at an early age as, according to Plotkin. [96] The notion that if we experience environmental destruction we'll identify with our environment[92] has made me wonder about the impact of what we label *natural disaster*. If we view the rest of the natural world as our equal, then we're not only going to care for the environment when oil spills mar the beauty of a region, we're going to care for the environment as we care for ourselves in the process of rebuilding after massive storms.

I identified with the Flinders Chase National Park when I saw the charred remains that blanketed the area in 2009. I was also sad to see the destruction left by a particularly violent storm around the Mataranka thermal springs. Trees were strewn everywhere as if a bulldozer had plowed everything in its path. Hope blossomed in the silence of contemplation as the landscape of Flinders Chase formed blankets of vegetation that attracted various animals back to the region. The greatest marvel was the process of regeneration; life didn't end, but rose to the challenge. Looking to nature reminds me that I am not alone and I can be resilient in the face of great difficulty.

THE GREAT WORK

In *The Great Work,* Thomas Berry writes about ethics by telling the story of the creation of the universe and how people fit in.[97] As a historical guide, Berry points out that the European occupation of North America had admirable intentions, but essentially assaulted the indigenous people and looted the land.[97] To the colonizers the land was something to be exploited "and brought under human and Christian discipline."[97] According to Berry, the Europeans had no idea of the "devastation they were causing" by suppressing "the way of life of...indigenous peoples" or by introducing them to diseases and disturbing the ecosystems with "commercial-industrial obsessions."[97] Kathleen Harrison wrote in *Moonrise* that "unconscious use of anything is damaging, and conscious use of anything can make it medicine."[98]

I am reminded once more of the story of the Christian medical missionaries and how they criticized indigenous medicine as lacking a scientific foundation while also suggesting that it could be used to create new means of treatment.[99] As a result of unconscious devastation, "the Great Work now...is to carry out the transition from a period of human devastation of the Earth to a period when humans would be present to the planet in a mutually beneficial manner." This would include giving "other-than-human modes of being rights, reality, and value beyond their benefits to humans" so that they can "be themselves and...express their own inner qualities."[97]

How we care for the earth matters because "a healing of the Earth is a prerequisite for the healing of the human." We can only survive "as long as we can breathe the air of Earth, drink its waters, and be nourished by its foods."[97] This sentiment is not new. The Earth Charter, an initiative for sustainable development, states that we should be guided by a moral code of action in order to recognize that 'every form of life is unique, warranting respect regardless of its worth to man."[100] These ideas aid in reminding us that because we are a part of an interrelated web of life, by caring for the rest of the natural world we are caring for ourselves.

Berry suggests that we refrain from renouncing ownership of our role in participating in a sustainable relationship with nature since taking ownership is for the "benefit of the larger community as well as ourselves." It occurs to me that our responsibility to future generations is to count them among our community, show our concern for them, and honor our responsibility to them as future co-inhabitants by giving them "some sense of the Great Work." Just as care for the rest of the natural world is a way of caring for ourselves, caring for future generations—not to mention modeling that care—also teaches us to look beyond our lifetime and recognize that "no age lives completely unto itself."[97] This also suggests that we periodically go back and review the Great Work, our personal work, as well as the ethical standards to which we agree. Doing so will help us be mindful of what we value and adjust when times, circumstances, and resources change.

If the idea of taking responsibility for future generations seems daunting, consider it from a personal perspective. If the Great Work is for all of us to do, what is your part? Personal work is what Jean Shinoda Bolen would call an assignment that feels like it has your name on it. [101] It is meaningful to you. Your "personal work needs to be aligned with the Great Work."[97] If we're all aligned with the Great Work, then I would suggest, a basic ethical standard can help ensure we're all headed in the same direction, regardless of which path we travel. We must also identify our part in the Great Work because, as social and environmental writer Terry Tempest Williams points out, we cannot "look for leadership beyond ourselves and wait for someone or something to save us from our global predicaments and obligations."[98] Our primary concern, by aligning with the Great Work, is to restore the "organic economy" of the planet by practicing reciprocity and inclusion so that we give as we receive and recognize that "all are needed."[97] Through reciprocity we create a sustainable relationship and through inclusion we bring about diversity which, according to Nina Simons, recognizes the value and wisdom that is found in nature's complexity, and provides a survival strategy by providing us with the opportunity to adapt and become resilient in this time of change[98]

TRACKING ARTEMIS

Artemis can serve as a guide for both a strategy for survival and a code of conduct for ecopsychology. 'Artemeas' means 'Safe and Sound' which refers to her role of protecting "those who were threatened."[102] If all are needed, in the case of diversity, then by protecting those that are threatened we, by extension, protect ourselves.

By the same token, Artemis was not perfect. She was known to be "quick to act in anger" which caused harm.[102] If we know that we have similar tendencies, we can account for our behaviors by recognizing and avoiding what triggers us so that we don't fall into harmful patterns of behavior. If we, for example, assumed the role of medical missionary and took the Hippocratic Oath (Appendix G) we'd be committing to work according to our "greatest ability and judgment" so that we would "do no harm or injustice" to those we consider our patients or those we are working with as a part of our mission. This means we not only protect those who are threatened, we agree to do our best in our relationship with the rest of the organic economy even if that means we limit the threat we pose.

THE DIVINE FEMININE

Returning to the insights born of the Artemis metaphor, it is important to note that she was also part of a whole: she was twin sister to Apollo, female to his male, moon to his sun.[102] Artemis is relevant as a metaphor for ecopsychology because she represents the feminine and the call, as with the Great Work, is to move away from dominance into a time of nurturance. This is not about gender, but a way of being. In her contributions to *Moonrise* Terry Tempest Williams noted that moving from dominance to nurturance is a "way of being in the world through presence and instinct and the courage that comes from falling in love with the earth."[98] Instead of dominance, if we follow the path outlined by Nina Simons in the same book, we "listen actively and inwardly, reach across the differences that tend to divide us, initiate and choose the hard work of collaboration, stay connected with our passion, and inspire enthusiastic engagement to strengthen and catalyze others into action."[98]

As an example of bringing together the feminine and masculine aspects of ourselves, we can look to Artemis as a huntress. Her weapon of choice was the bow and arrow.[102] More than a hunting tool, the bow and arrow have spiritual aspects that connect the Sicangu-Lakota tribe to their environment. The bow, according to tribe member Joseph Marshall III, came from the new moon and the arrow is as "straight as the arrows of the sun."[104] This illustrates that we can learn practical things by looking to our environment and can find wholeness when we bring together the moon and the sun, the feminine and the masculine. [104]

THE WILDS

Artemis was also a maiden who put a high value on purity.[102] She would guard her virginity and punish those who did not maintain theirs, even if they had been raped. *Wilds* and *wilderness*, in this context, could be defined as *untouched* or *virgin nature*.

Artemis became Goddess of the Wilds or Goddess of the Wilderness because of her "preference for being out in the wilds."[102] Recognizing that Artemis protects those that are threatened, I found it compelling that she was a huntress and yet "wild animals were said to become tame" or would "behave as if they were tame" when they were in her temple. I attributed this behavior to the understanding the animals had that they would be protected within those boundaries. If this was the case then protection could be seen as reciprocity where Artemis recognized that "whoever receives must also give"[97] so that those who receive time to hunt must also give animals time away from hunting. Protection, in this instance, could also literally mean *untouched* where the animals were not to be harmed or threatened.

PROTECT THE YOUNG

Protection can be viewed as a principle of conservation because in protecting the young we also need to protect their mothers, which means hunting or harming female animals "could have fatal consequences"[97] in relation to future hunting seasons. Artemis recognizes the role of youth because, in addition to representing protection, the name 'Artemis Korythalia' means "the flowering of young branches, and may refer either to the growth of vegetation or metaphorically to the growth of children."[102] By protecting young animals we allow them the chance to mature and our children the chance to know them directly.

As an example the Gullah Geechee people operate from the standpoint that there is enough for everyone. As a result, everyone takes only what he or she needs without a sense of ownership.[90] The depletion of shrimp and blue crab from around the Sea Islands is attributed to outsiders overfishing and taking the female crabs before they could lay their eggs.[90] By failing to protect those we rely upon for nourishment, we limit what is available.

In thinking of protection, I cannot help but consider Artemis' pride in her skills as a huntress.[102] With regards to a code of ethics for ecopsychology, I appreciate the seeming irony of protecting the wilderness while killing the animals that inhabit it. By examining the myth of Artemis I have been able to recognize that with her skills as a huntress comes an understanding of the sacred value of life. By protecting mothers, the young, and the lame, hunting becomes truly about skill and necessity, not profane mass destruction. There is an honoring of life in how Artemis conducted herself, and in that I am reminded of the story of Antelope.

THE GIFT OF ANTELOPE

According to indigenous teachings, Antelope is about action. [105] The Great Mystery sent Antelope to People, who were nearly extinct. The intent was to teach them "to do" because if there is action there is no reason to fear. People asked what to do with their naked, hungry selves and Antelope offered, as a gift, his coat for warmth and his flesh for hunger.[105] While "action is the key and essence of living," the story of Antelope also illustrates life's circle through the offering of one life so that others may live.[105] This story has led me to realize that it is not just up to humans to protect those that are threatened. Any life, like Antelope, can answer the call for protection in an organic economy.

ETHICAL MARKERS

At this point in the journey I have continued to follow the bear as a guide for the considerations of ethical standards for ecopsychology, and discovered the Goddess of the Wilderness. Through Artemis, I have found a metaphor for ethics that recognizes the importance of protecting the vulnerable, guarding against our own temper, and seeing ourselves as part of a whole. With Christian missionaries as guides I have found the need to limit comparisons of culture or lifestyle so that the person carrying out the mission is not in the position of judging another as inferior. To stay true to our organic economy and our profession we must remember to prioritize serving life and society over technology and industry. We also do not exist in isolation so the culture of both the participants and the missionary will have an influence through impressions people have of each other or the procedure that is followed.

The Code

This is a journey of discovery.

During this leg of the journey I noticed that the train I was riding on stopped before crossing an aging bridge. Sailors wanted to pass in order to commemorate the unofficial start to the Seattle summer: July 5th. When we stopped, the sun shone directly in my face.

I continued to write as time lapsed. I was not aware of the moment when the sun was no longer directly on me. How often do we, you and me, stop yet still fail to notice a moment until it has passed?

I am already saddened with the realization that with each passing day, we see the sun less and less, yet in this moment, it clings to the horizon as a deep red ball on a clear day.

Shades of blue darken around me, dancing with hues of pink and red. Fields of green stretch beside me, creating a corridor from Stanwood to Bellingham, a dividing line between sun and sky, day and night, until the sun is no more.

Before long, all that is left is a fading from pale blue and orange to the darkness of the land. As dusk settles in and then disappears we glide along the water, reflecting the light of the world as we gently roll along our chosen path.

Chapter 5:

The Value of the Journey

At the outset of this journey, I had not looked up the definition of ethics. It was through the survey of literature that I realized what I sought was a code of conduct, a guideline for my behavior, and a focus for my work. My search for appropriate guidelines evolved to include definitions and the code of ethics for psychology. While the idea of freedom of choice resonates with me, I've also realized that my process did not account for how my work could stigmatize the missionary community. Consequently, I can now appreciate how easy it can be to believe that one is on the side of *what is right* in the name of *protection for others.*

Based on everything I've read, written, and thought about, a code of ethics for my practice, ecopsychology, and those looking to have a more intentional relationship with the rest of the natural world should:

- Be inclusive and compassionate rather than threatening, superior, judgmental
- Ensure that every life form is respected regardless of its worth to our mission or humankind
- Look beyond our generation
- Plan and work on behalf of the natural world
- Measure and account for any damage or devastation our mission might cause
- Honor the law of reciprocity where we give what we receive and uphold that all life forms have worth
- Promote diversity as nature's strategy for adaptation and resilience in the face of change

- Consult the principles of ecopsychology to determine whether our work suits a given mission
- Practice mindfulness and be slow to make judgments about others
- Consider the global context, not just the individual one
- Treat each person/life in a way that respects their inherent divinity
- Offer information/suggestions without attaching expectations to them
- Afford each person/life the freedom or intrinsic right to be different
- Prioritize serving life and society to things and technology
- Consider and account for the history, cultures, traditions, roles, and religions of the people/life involved in our mission
- Account for our culture and the culture of those with whom we are interacting
- Account for the social contexts of society, practice, faith
- Give priority to protecting the poor, oppressed, exploited and marginalized

Many of these items will need to be more specifically defined so that they are more precise in guiding our behavior. This is only an outline because it is my hope that this book will serve as a springboard for further discussion about where ecopsychology is headed and what must be done to get there. Specifics may change and evolve as the field and its disciplines learn and grow, but the outline can provide a foundation on which to build.

As ecopsychology brings together several areas of study, I thought it would also be sensible to look at the code of ethics for related fields such as ecology, psychology, and environmentalism (Appendix B, C, D). Those fields alluded to abstaining from discriminating or harassing others as well as striving for honesty, objectivity, and well-defined boundaries in reporting and obtaining credit for one's work. This is particularly significant in considering that these professions, like ecopsychology, can be quoted in media and their theories can have a "direct effect on the public."[107]

I noticed that the code of ethics for ecology mentions certification as a way to bring about accountability. What I like about the idea of certification is that it can include an oath, like the Ethics of Apprenticeship (Appendix I), that can serve as a personal reminder of the work to be done and the relationships to be created. The code for environmentalism was notably different from the others in that it asked professionals to account for the needs of the natural world. This allowed for a more pointed reminder to consider our relationship to the rest of the natural world, which was not something I picked up on in the other codes.

In the end, while the code of ethics for psychology can cover ecopsychology, It seems to me that it does not provide enough coverage for a field labeled *area of interest* that focuses on our relationship with the rest of the earth. An addendum to psychology's code of ethics could suffice, but an entirely separate code of conduct would give ecopsychology both the literal and figurative distance to evaluate individual and collective responsibilities to earth.

The Work We're to Do

For E. O. Wilson, the work we are all here to do involves a "decision of ethics, how we value the natural world."[108] While ethical standards help to ensure that we make informed decisions in terms of understanding what we are to retain in our growth process and what we are to give up, the work that must be done is no small feat. Being in service to life requires that we be mindful of the need for protection while also realizing that as awareness is raised, people may have emotional responses such as grief. We may grieve for our part in the past and our load for the future. Grief can be helpful. It can provide a needed release and bring us into the present, a place where we can prepare for change.

Another way to look at this is if awareness is the "painful process of removing the scab," then grieving is the "the healing balm of attention, love, and forgiveness."[106] If, for example, we have a favorite place from our childhood and we return to find it's changed in ways that sadden us, we may grieve by sharing memories of how things used to be or why they mattered to us. As we grieve in this way, we can serve as a model for the generations we parent. What we model doesn't have to be *this could happen to you* but that *our environment, our places matter.*

Just as change is more likely to be temporary if a person feels forced into action, awareness cannot be rushed. Ecopsychology, as a response to both environmentalism and psychology, recognizes that you "cannot impose change on other people. It is just like nature. If we want rain to come, we must plant trees."[106] Planting trees changes the soil, the atmosphere, and contributes to the entire cycle of life. If we plant the idea that we can do our part to make a difference and that takes root, what sprouts will more likely be a sustaining motivation for participating in the life cycle. If, instead, we plant a demand for action and water it with shame and blame, what sprouts will more likely wither and return to the soil rather than blossom into participation.

What we do changes our relationship to the rest of life. As trees can attest, growth happens slowly. It is important to know that "broken places are our new frontiers."[106] As we reconnect or restore our relationship with the rest of the natural world it is not enough to know that the natural world has value, we must also see that we are a part of the natural world and that we also have value. The new frontier, for some of us, may be realizing that everything we do is a balance of needs for ourselves, our family, and our natural community.

It is also not enough to know or understand a code of conduct for ourselves; we must share our code and the reasons why it matters. This is no different than our ancestors teaching "the traditional ways of celebrating, harvesting, and sharing wild foods."[106] Even Jumping Mouse returned to his community to tell them about the Sacred River.[109]

Sharing is not limited. The story and the honoring of Artemis continued through song and dance. She, herself, was so good at performing that at one point she was said to cause a "day to lengthen" when Helios, the sun god, stopped to "watch her dance in the mid-summer."[110] Sharing is how knowledge and understanding are spread. You educate a community when you educate a girl because even in villages she will share what she knows at the local watering hole. People survive because Antelope shared the secret of action then shared his life so that they could be fed and kept warm.[111]

As you move forward from this journey, what will you do differently? If your answer is 'nothing,' then you should know that "your inactions are as much a part of shaping the world as the actions of others."[106] It would be just as significant if our ancestors had *not* chosen to set aside wilderness territory like Yellowstone, Yosemite, and the Adirondack Forest Preserve.[108]

As professionals, we must adhere to the ethical standards that are ratified by governing bodies. As individuals, we are able to choose what we wish to incorporate and what we will leave behind. In this sense, we are like Red Jacket the Seneca who told the missionaries that he'd wait to see how those who were converted acted, before deciding to convert to Christianity himself.[108] In the face of climate change, global warming, and the increased frequency of extreme storms, it feels safe to note that "our present Earth is not the Earth as it always was and always will be."[108] The question is what will we do about it?

Epilogue

Since writing the original paper, I have a better context for applying an ethical standard. Going back and revisiting some ideas and books has been like recertifying in wilderness first aid or first responder training. Initially, I could not envision how the skills I was learning would be used. Upon recertification I had participated in and apprenticed on a wilderness quest so the course content seemed easier. For ethics, I could only imagine how a code of conduct would work since my classes did not include training in psychotherapy or any direct work with clients. It wasn't until I realized I could apply my knowledge through personal coaching that I found both a context for applying an ethical standard and a profession that already had one (Appendix H).

A blog post I wrote called *Consent*[112] illustrates what I've learned. In it I note that asking someone permission to coach them or treat them as a wilderness first responder is a sign of respect. This enables the potential client to provide consent and empowers the individual with the ability to choose. In this, a partnership is born. I then considered what it would be like if we sought consent from the rest of the natural world before we approached, entered, or took even so much as a pebble. It would, like in coaching or wilderness first aid, show respect and allow for a co-created experience. On my wilderness quest my mentor had me introduce myself to the environment and ask permission to be there. With that shift in dynamic I was more attuned to the fact that the environment could let me know that I wasn't welcome. Instead, I felt at ease once I introduced myself because my attention was drawn to a nearby purple flower. Purple is my favorite color. Believing I had permission to be present, I continued to follow where my attention led me and that resulted in a powerful partnership that will be a story for another time.

References

"Perhaps you have come to this place, to this moment, to these people, to this challenge, for just such a time as this." MORDECAI TO ESTHER, IN THE BOOK OF RUTH.[113]

REFERENCES PREFACE

1. Hansen, J. (2009). *Storms of my grandchildren; the truth about the coming climate catastrophe and our last chance to save humanity.* New York, NY: Bloomsbury

2. Ibarra, H. (2004). *Working Identity: Unconventional strategies for reinventing your career.* Boston, MA: Harvard Business School Press

3. Associated Press. (January 21, 2012). Highlights from President Obama's inaugural speech. Retrieved from http://news.msn.com/politics/highlights-from-president-obamas-inaugural-speech

4. Maddow, R & Cuomo, A. (November 1, 2012). *Extreme weather is here to stay.* Retrieved from The Rachel Maddow Show web site: http://www.msnbc.msn.com/id/26315908/vp/49652299#49652299

5. Kelly, S. (1993). The path of place. In F. Hull (Ed.), *Earth and spirit; the spiritual dimension of the environmental crisis* (pp. 105-113). New York, NY: The Continuum Publishing Company

6. Watkins, M. (2009). Creating restorative ecotherapeutic practices. In L. Buzzell, & C. Chalquist (Eds.), *Ecotherapy; healing with nature in mind* (pp. 219-236). San Francisco, CA: Sierra Club Books

7. Smith, D. B. (2010, January 31). Is there an ecological unconscious? *The New York Times*

8. Dedeaux, T. A. (2009, December 24). *Ecopsychology and the Experience of Grief and Loss.* Retrieved from http://voices.yahoo.com/ecopsychology-experience-grief-loss-5132555.html?cat=9

9. Prochaska, J. O., Norcross, J.C., & Diclemente, Carlo C. (2010). *Changing for good: A revolutionary six-stage program for overcoming bad habits and moving your life positively forward.* New York, NY: HarperCollins

10. Dedeaux, T. A. (2011). *Rooted in water: the importance of story to ecopsychology and the beginning of a practice in narrative ecopsychology.* Seattle, WA: CreateSpace

11. Roszak, T. (2001, December 23). When the counterculture counted. *SF Gate.* Retrieved from http://www.sfgate.com/books/article/When-the-counterculture-counted-2835958.php#ixzz2INS9lQkl

12. Roszak, T. (1992, 2001). *The voice of the earth: an exploration of ecopsychology* (2nd ed.). Grand Rapids, MI: Phanes Press, Inc.

13. Mack, J. E. (1995). The politics of species arrogance. In T. Roszak, M. E. Gomes, & A. D. Kanner (Eds.), *Ecopsychology: Restoring the earth, healing the*

mind (pp. 279-287). San Francisco, CA: Sierra Club Books

14. Stewart, E. C., & Bennett, M. J. (1991). *American cultural patterns: A cross-cultural perspective* (Revised ed.). Yarmouth, ME: Intercultural Press, Inc.

15. Ferguson, G. (2009). *Shouting at the sky: Troubled teens and the promise of the wild* (Paperback ed.). New York, NY: Sweetgrass Books

REFERENCES CHAPTER 1

16. Andrew, T. (1993). *Animal speak: the spiritual & magical powers of creatures great & small.* St. Paul, MN: Llewellyn Publications

17. Dedeaux, T. A. (2011). *Rooted in water: the importance of story to ecopsychology and the beginning of a practice in narrative ecopsychology.* Seattle, WA: CreateSpace

18. Roszak, T. (1992, 2001). *The voice of the earth: an exploration of ecopsychology* (2nd ed.). Grand Rapids, MI: Phanes Press, Inc.

19. Symonds, G. W. (1958). *The tree identification book.* New York, NY: HarperCollins Publishers Inc.

20. Brown, L. R. (1995). Ecopsychology and the environmental revolution. In T. Roszak, M. E. Gomes, & A. D. Kanner (Eds.), *Ecopsychology; restoring the earth, healing the mind.* San Francisco, CA: Sierra Club Books

21. Cohen, M. J. (2000, August). *Nature connected psychology: creating moments that let earth teach.* (M. Press, Editor, & International Community of Ecopsychology) Retrieved November 10, 2009, from Gatherings: seeking ecopsychology:

http://www.ecopsychology.org/journal/gathering s3/cohen.html

22. Roszak, T. (1995). Where psyche meets gaia. In T. Roszak, M. E. Gomes, & A. D. Kanner (Eds.), *Ecopsychology; restoring the earth, healing the mind.* San Francisco: Sierra Club Books

23. Harper, D. (2001, November). Retrieved January 24, 2010, from Online etymology dictionary: http://www.etymonline.com/

24. Drengson, A., & Devall, B. (Eds.). (2008). *The ecology of wisdom; writings by arne naess.* Berkeley, CA: Counterpoint

25. Fisher, A. (2002). *Radical ecopsychology; psychology in the service of life.* Albany, NY: State University of New York Press

26. Encyclopedia Britannica. (2010). Retrieved January 24, 2010, from Britannica.com: http://www.britannica.com/

27. Shepard, P. (1995). Nature and madness. In T. Roszak, M. E. Gomes, & A. D. Kanner (Eds.), *Ecopsychology; restoring the earth, healing the mind.* San Francisco: Sierra Club Books

28. Goodall, J. (1999). Foreword. In T. Roszak, *The gendered atom; reflections on the sexual psychology of science.* Berkeley, CA: Conari Press

29. Fisher, A. (2002). *Radical ecopsychology; psychology in the service of life.* Albany, NY: State University of New York Press

30. The American Heritage Dictionary of the English Language (2009). Retrieved January 24, 2010, from Dictionary.com: http://dictionary.reference.com/

31. Encyclopedia Britannica. (2010). *Environmentalism.* Retrieved January 24, 2010, from Britannica.com:

http://www.britannica.com/EBchecked/topic/189 205/environmentalism

32. Hillman, J. (1995). A psyche the size of the earth. In T. Roszak, M. E. Gomes, & A. D. Kanner (Eds.), *Ecopsychology; restoring the earth, healing the mind.* San Francisco: Sierra Club Books

33. Roszak, T. (1999). The gendered atom; reflections on the sexual psychology of science. Berkeley, CA: Conari Press

34. Sewall, L. (1995). The skill of ecological perception. In T. Roszak, M. E. Gomes, & A. D. Kanner (Eds.), *Ecopsychology; restoring the earth, healing the mind.* San Francisco: Sierra Club Books

35. Liebert, R. M., & Liebert, L. L. (1988). *Personality strategies and issues* (8th Edition ed.). Pacific Grove, CA: Brooks / Cole Publishing Company

36. Schroll, M. A. (2007). Wrestling with Arne Naess: A Chronicle of Ecopsychology's Origins. *The Trumpeter , 23* (1)

37. Brody, H. (2000). *The other side of eden.* Vancouver, BC, Canada: Douglas & McIntyre

REFERENCES CHAPTER 2

38. Some', M. P. (1994). *Of water and the spirit: Ritual, magic, and initiation in the life of an African shaman.* New York, NY: Penguin Compass

39. Brody, H. (2000). *The other side of eden: Hunters, farmers, and the shaping of the world.* New York City, NY: North Point Press

40. Dedeaux, T. A. (2012, October 18). A return to life. Retrieved from http://narrativeecopsych.wordpress.com/2012/1 0/18/a-return-to-life/

41. Dedeaux, T. A. (2012, May 6). The wilderness makes you smarter. Retrieved from http://narrativeecopsych.wordpress.com/2012/05/06/the-wilderness-makes-you-smarter/

42. Klingle, M. (2007). *Emerald city: An environmental history of Seattle.* New Haven & London: Yale University Press

43. Meadows, D. H. (2008). *Thinking in systems: A primer.* White River Junction, VT: Chelsea Green Publishing Company

44. Dedeaux, T. A. (2011). Rooted in water: the importance of story to ecopsychology and the beginning of a practice in narrative ecopsychology. Seattle, WA: CreateSpace

45. (2010). (Dictionary.com, LLC) Retrieved October 29, 2010, from Dictionary.com: http://dictionary.reference.com/

46. Harper, D. (2001, November). Retrieved January 24, 2010, from Online etymology dictionary: http://www.etymonline.com/

47. Fredrickson, L. M., & Anderson, D. H. (1999). A qualitative exploration of the wilderness experience as a source of spiritual inspiration. Journal of Environmental Psychology , 19 (1), 21-39

48. Rudzitis, G., & Johansen, H. E. (1991). How important is wilderness? Results from a United States survey. Environmental Management , XV (2), 227-233

49. Gustafson, F. (1997). Dancing between two worlds: Jung and the native American soul. Mahwah, NJ: Paulist Press

50. Kim, U., Yang, K. Hwang, K. eds. (2006) Indigenous and Cultural Psychology, Understanding people in context. New York, NY: Springer Science

51. Ferguson, G. (1999). Shouting at the sky: Troubled teens and the promise of the wild. New York, NY: Thomas Dunne Books

52. Tarnas, R. (2001). *Is the modern psyche undergoing a rite of passage?* Retrieved October 11, 2010, from Cosmos and Psyche: http://www.cosmosandpsyche.com/pdf/Revision RiteofPassage.pdf

53. Foster, S. and Little, M. (1992). The book of the vision quest: Personal transformation in the wilderness. New York, NY: Simon and Schuster

54. Plotkin, B. (2003). Soulcraft: Crossing into the mysteries of nature and psyche. Novato, CA: New World Library

55. Macy, J. (2008, February 1). *The greatest danger.* Retrieved November 1, 2009, from Yes magazine: http://yesmagazine.org/issues/climate-solutions/the-greatest-danger

56. Bochner, S. (2003). *Culture schock due to contact with unfamiliar cultures.* Retrieved October 6, 2010, from Online readings in psychology and culture: http://www.ac.wwu.edu/~culture/Bochner.htm

57. Sussman, N. M. (2002). *Sojourners to another country: the psychological roller-coaster of cultural transitions.* Retrieved October 6, 2010, from Online readings in psychology and culture: http://www.ac.wwu.edu/~culture/sussman.htm

58. Suh, E. M., & Oishi, S. (2002). *Subjective well-being across cultures.* (W. J. Lonner, D. L. Dinnel, S. A. Hayes, & D. N. Sattler, Editors) Retrieved September 23, 2010, from Online readings in

psychology and culture:
http://www.ac.wwu.edu/~culture/Suh_Oishi.htm

59. Altarriba, J., Basnight, D. M., & Canary, T. M. (2003). *Emotion representation and perception across cultures.* Retrieved October 6, 2010, from Online readings in psychology and culture:
http://www.ac.wwu.edu/~culture/altarriba2.htm

60. Brown, L. R. (1995). Ecopsychology and the environmental revolution. In T. Roszak, M. E. Gomes, & A. D. Kanner (Eds.), *Ecopsychology; restoring the earth, healing the mind.* San Francisco, CA: Sierra Club Books

61. Andrews, T. (1993). *Animal speak: The spiritual & magical powers of creatures great and small.* Woodbury, MN: Llewellyn Publications

REFERENCES CHAPTER 3

62. Foster, S., & Little, M. (1989). *The roaring of the sacred river: The wilderness quest for vision and self-healing.* New York, NY: Prentice Hall Press

63. Andrews, T. (1993). *Animal speak: The spiritual & magical powers of creatures great and small.* Woodbury, MN: Llewellyn Publications

64. D'Este, S. (2005). *Artemis: Virgin goddess of the sun & moon.* England, UK: Avalonia

65. Shinoda Bolen, J. (2001). *Goddesses in older women: Archetypes in women over fifty.* New York, NY: HarperCollins Publishers Inc.

66. Campbell, J., & Moyers, B. D. (1988). *The power of myth.* New York, NY: Anchor Books

67. Davis, W. (Performer). (2003, February). *Endangered cultures.* Long Beach, CA. Available

from:
http://www.ted.com/talks/lang/eng/wade_davis_
on_endangered_cultures.html

68. Schaefer, C. (2006). *Grandmothers counsel the world.* Boston, MA: Trumpeter Books

69. Shepard, P. (1995). Nature and madness. In T. G. Roszak, *Ecopsychology, restoring the earth healing the mind.* (p. 34). San Francisco: Sierra Club Books

70. Berry, T. (1999). *The great work: Our way into the future.* New York, NY: Bell Tower

71. Beauregard, M., & O'Leary, D. (2007). The spiritual brain: A neuroscientist's case for the existence of the soul. New York, NY: Harper One

72. Cahalan, W. (1995). Ecological groundedness in gestalt theory. In T. Roszak, M. E. Gomes, & A. D. Kanner (Eds.), *Ecopsychology: Restoring the earth, healing the mind* (pp. 216-223). San Francisco, CA: Sierra Club Books

73. Maathai, W. (2010). Replenishing the earth: Spiritual values for healing ourselves and. New York, NY: Random House, Inc.

74. Stalnaker, A. (2008). Judging others; History, ethics, and the purposes of comparison. *The Journal of Religious Ethics, Inc. , 36* (3), pp. 425-444

75. Hansen, J. (2009). *Storms of my grandchildren; the truth about the coming climate catastrophe and our last chance to save humanity.* New York, NY: Bloomsbury

76. Campbell, G. G. (2010, September). Review of Nature Ethics by Marti Kheel. *Ecopsychology , 2* (3), pp. 195-198

77. Some', M. P. (1994). *Of water and the spirit: Ritual, magic, and initiation in the life of an African shaman.* New York, NY: Penguin Compass

78. Stanley, B. (2009). Mission and human identity in the light of Edinburgh 1910. *Mission Studies*, *26*, pp. 80-97

79. Bowen, W. R. (2010). Ethics and the engineer: Developing the basis of a theological approach. *Studies in Christian Ethics*, *23* (3), pp. 227-248

80. Roszak, T. (1998). *Ecopsychology: Eight principles.* Retrieved January 11, 2010, from Ecopsychology on-line: Introducing ecopsychology: http://ecopsychology.athabascau.ca/Final/intro.htm

81. Roszak, T. (1992, 2001). *The voice of the earth: an exploration of ecopsychology* (2nd ed.). Grand Rapids, MI: Phanes Press, Inc.

82. Pfister, L. (2005). Protestant ethics among Chinese missionaries, problems of indigenization, and the spirit of academic professionalization. *Journal of Classical Sociology*, *5* (1), pp. 93-114

83. Hokkanen, M. (2004). Scottish missionaries and African healers: Perceptions and relations in the Livingstonia Mission, 1875-1930. *Journal of Religion in Africa*, *34* (3), pp. 320-347

84. Banyard, P., & Flanagan, C. (2005). *Ethical issues and guidelines in psychology.* New York, NY: Routledge Taylor & Francis Group

85. Macy, J. (2008, February 1). *The greatest danger.* Retrieved November 1, 2009, from Yes magazine: http://yesmagazine.org/issues/climate-solutions/the-greatest-danger

REFERENCES CHAPTER 4

86. Roszak, T., Gomes, M.E., & Kanner, A.D. (Eds.). (1995). *Ecopsychology: Restoring the earth, healing the mind*. San Francisco, CA: Sierra Club Books

87. Tarnas, R. (2001). *Is the modern psyche undergoing a rite of passage?* Retrieved October 11, 2010, from Cosmos and Psyche: http://www.cosmosandpsyche.com/pdf/Revision RiteofPassage.pdf

88. Campbell, J., & Moyers, B. D. (1988). *The power of myth*. New York, NY: Anchor Books

89. Ray, P. H., & Anderson, S. R. (2000). The cultural creatives: How 50 million people are changing the world. New York, NY: Harmony Books

90. Dedeaux, T. A. (2011). *Rooted in water: the importance of story to ecopsychology and the beginning of a practice in narrative ecopsychology.* Seattle, WA: CreateSpace

91. Liebert, R. M., & Liebert, L. L. (1998). *Personality: Strategies and issues* (8th ed.). Pacific Grove, CA: Brooks/Cole Publishing Company

92. Clayton, S., & Myers, G. (2009). *Conservation psychology: Understanding and promoting human care for nature.* Hoboken, NJ: Wiley-Blackwell

93. Fisher, A. (2002). *Radical ecopsychology; psychology in the service of life.* Albany, NY: State University of New York Press

94. West, R. (2007). Out of the shadow: Ecopsychology, story, and encounters with the land. Charlottesville, VA: University of Virginia Press

95. Plotkin, B. (2008). *Nature and the human soul.* Novato, CA: New World Library

96. Clayton, S. & Opotow, S. (Eds.). (2003). *Identity and the natural environment: the psychological*

significance of nature. United States of America: Massachusetts Institute of Technology

97. Berry, T. (1999). *The great work: Our way into the future.* New York, NY: Bell Tower

98. Simons, N. & Campbell, A. (Eds.). (2010). *Moonrise: The Power of Women Leading from the Heart.* Rochester, VT: Park Street Press

99. Hokkanen, M. (2004). Scottish missionaries and African healers: Perceptions and relations in the Livingstonia Mission, 1875-1930. *Journal of Religion in Africa , 34* (3), pp. 320-347

100.   The Earth Charter Initiative. (2008). *The earth charter.* Retrieved from http://www.earthcharterinaction.org/content/pages/Read-the-Charter.html

101.   Shinoda Bolen, J. (2001). *Goddesses in older women: Archetypes in women over fifty.* New York, NY: HarperCollins Publishers Inc.

102.   D'Este, S. (2005). *Artemis: Virgin goddess of the sun & moon.* England, UK: Avalonia

103.   Roszak, T. (1992, 2001). *The voice of the earth: an exploration of ecopsychology* (2nd ed.). Grand Rapids, MI: Phanes Press, Inc.

104.   Martin, M. & Marshall III, J. (November 2, 2012). *Lakota spiritual guidance from the bow and arrow.* Retrieved http://www.npr.org/2012/11/02/164178390/lakota-spiritual-guidance-from-the-bow-and-arrow

105.   Sams, J., & Carson, D. (1988). Medicine cards; the discovery of power through the ways of animals. San Fe, NM: Bear & Company

REFERENCES CHAPTER 5

106.   Simons, N. & Campbell, A. (Eds.). (2010). *Moonrise: The Power of Women Leading from the Heart.* Rochester, VT: Park Street Press

107.   Banyard, P., & Flanagan, C. (2005). *Ethical issues and guidelines in psychology.* New York, NY: Routledge Taylor & Francis Group

108.   Berry, T. (1999). *The great work: Our way into the future.* New York, NY: Bell Tower

109.   Foster, S., & Little, M. (1989). *The roaring of the sacred river: The wilderness quest for vision and self-healing.* New York, NY: Prentice Hall Press

110.   D'Este, S. (2005). *Artemis: Virgin goddess of the sun & moon.* England, UK: Avalonia

111.   Sams, J., & Carson, D. (1988). Medicine cards; the discovery of power through the ways of animals. San Fe, NM: Bear & Company

REFERENCES EPILOGUE

112.   Dedeaux, T. A. (2012, June 12). *Consent.* Retrieved from http://narrativeecopsych.wordpress.com/2012/06/12/consent/

REFERENCES

113.   Simons, N. & Campbell, A. (Eds.). (2010). *Moonrise: The Power of Women Leading from the Heart.* Rochester, VT: Park Street Press

REFERENCES APPENDIX

114.   Meadows, D. H. (2008). *Thinking in systems: A primer.* White River Junction, VT: Chelsea Green Publishing Company

Bibliography

Adichie, C. (Performer). (2009, July). *The danger of the single story.* United States of America

Burns, G. W. (1998). *Nature-guided therapy: Brief integrative strategies for health and well-being.* Philadelphia, PA: Brunner/Mazel

Chalquist, C. (2009). A look at the ecotherapy research evidence. *Ecopsychology , 1* (2)

Clinebell, H. (1996). *Ecotherapy: Healing ourselves, healing the earth.* Minneapolis, MN: Augsburg Fortress

Cohen, M. J. (2000, August). *Nature connected psychology: creating moments that let earth teach.* (M. Press, Editor, & International Community of Ecopsychology) Retrieved November 10, 2009, from Gatherings: seeking ecopsychology: http://www.ecopsychology.org/journal/gatherings3/cohen.html

Dossey, L. M. (2009). The power of story: Observations from a book tour. *Explore , 5* (6), 309-312

Fisher, A. (2009). Ecopsychology as Radical Praxis. In L. Buzzell, & C. Chalquist (Eds.), *Ecotherapy; healing with nature in mind* (pp. 60-68). San Francisco, CA: Sierra Club Books

Fredrickson, L. M., & Anderson, D. H. (1999). A qualitative exploration of the wilderness experience as a source of spiritual inspiration. *Journal of Environmental Psychology , 19* (1), 21-39

Glotfelty, C., & Fromm, H. (Eds.). (1996). *The ecocriticism reader: Landmarks in literary ecology.* Athens, GA: University of Georgia Press

Hawken, P. (2007). *Blessed unrest: How the largest movement in the world came into being and why no one saw it coming.* London, England: Viking Penguin

Johnson, C. Y. (1998). A consideration of collective memory in African American attachment to wildland recreation places. *Research in Human Ecology, 5* (1), 5-15

Kahn, J. P., Severson, R. L., & Rockert, J. H. (2009). The human relation with nature and technological nature. *Association for Psychological Science, 18* (1), 37-42

Kapur, S. (Performer). (2009, November). *We are the stories we tell ourselves.* Mysore, India

Kelly, S. (1993). The path of place. In F. Hull (Ed.), *Earth and spirit; the spiritual dimension of the environmental crisis* (pp. 105-113). New York, NY: The Continuum Publishing Company

Klein, J. (Performer). (2010, February). *Photos that changed the world.* Long Beach, CA

Kumar, S., Deravy, E., & Kumar Mitchell, M. (2009). *Earth pilgrim.* Foxholle, Dartington, Totnes, Devon, UK: Green Books Ltd.

Labarre, S. (2010). *Infographic: What makes MLK's "I have a dream" speech brilliant.* (Mansuueto Ventures, LLC) Retrieved February 17, 2011, from Fastgodesign.com: http://www.fastcodesign.com/1663103/infographic-what-makes-mlks-i-have-a-dream-speech-brilliant

Lin. (2009). *Bear.* Retrieved from
http://www.linsdomain.com/totems/pages/bear.htm

Macy, J. (1991). *World as lover, world as self: Courage for global justice and ecological renewal.* Berkeley, CA: Parallax Press

Macy, J., & Young Brown, M. (1998). *Coming back to life: Practices to reconnect our lives, our world.* Gabriola Island, BC, Canada: New Society Publishers

McCarthy, A. (2012). *The longest way home: One man's quest for the courage to settle down.* New York, NY: Free Press

Nussbaum, T. (1998, November 23). *Ecopsychology: A combination of ecology, psychology, and religion.* Retrieved January 15, 2011, from Goshen.edu: http://www.goshen.edu/bio/Biol410/BSSPapers98/nussbaum.html

Rosalita, D. (Producer). (2004). *One voice, one love, one spirit: A sacred gathering* [Motion Picture]. Philadelphia, PA

Pattanaik, D. (Performer). (2009, November). *East versus West: The myths that mystify.* Mysore, India

Pinkola Estes, C. P. (1992, 1995). *Women who run with the wolves: Myths and stories of the wild woman archetype.* New York, NY: Ballantine Books

Rosalita, D. (Producer). (2003). *Rooted in water: The Gullah Geechee people* [Motion Picture]. Pittsburgh, PA

Rue, L. (2000). *Everybody's story: Wising up to the epic of evolution.* Albany, NY: State University of New York Press

Appendix

"Before you charge in to make things better, pay attention to the value of what's already there."

~ Donella H. Meadows[114]

A. Academic Paper
B. Ethics for Ecology
C. Ethics for Psychology
D. Ethics for Environmentalism
E. Ecopsychology Family Tree
F. Ten Commandments
G. Hippocratic Oath
H. Ethics for International Coaching Federation
I. Ethics of Apprenticeship
J. Leave No Trace

APPENDIX A:

ACADEMIC PAPER

Reading *Of Water and Spirit* by Malidoma Some'
(1994) caught my attention because Christianity was said
to be a contradiction as he experienced an attempt to
"tame" him in order to make him suitable for this society
(pp. 161, 167). The impact of Christian missionary work
on a native population came up for me again while I was
reading *The Other Side of Eden* by Hugh Brody (2000).
Brody immersed himself in the Native American culture of
Canada in order to help facilitate the assimilation of the
people into "civilized" society. Although Brody had the
goal of passing on "what hunter-gatherers can teach us not
only about their own particular human genius but also
about human history," conflict arose, and I was struck by
the loss of identity of the indigenous people as they were
discouraged from practicing their native ways (p. 6).

In reading these accounts of the impact Christian
missionary work on different indigenous populations, I

decided I would look into the ethics of the practice because I wanted to know what the ethical considerations were for spreading the gospel of Christianity, and if there is a positive way to engage in the practice so that the news continues to seem good to those who listen. I see the ethics of Christian missionary work as important to my own explorations in ecopsychology because if I am to tell people that they can be healthier and happier if they engage in a sustainable relationship with the natural world, I want to make sure that I do not violate – even unintentionally – the person that I am working with, or any protocols that should be in place.

INTRODUCTION

For the purposes of looking at the ethics of Christian missionary work, I am defining ethics as "the rules of conduct recognized in respect to a particular class of human actions or a particular group," and mission as "a group of persons sent by a church to carry on religious work [such as] evangelization in foreign lands, and often to establish schools, hospitals, etc." (Dictionary.com, 2010).

For further context I have found that in the 1590s a

mission was the "act of sending" members of the Jesuit

community abroad; it wasn't until the 1620s that a mission

was done with the intent do to some kind of business

(Harper, 2001). Evangelization, in turn, is the preaching of

the gospel and the conversion to Christianity. Although

conversion to Christianity is the goal of the missionary, I

am particularly curious to find out if the conversion is

willing or if the evangelizing is done in such a way as to be

respectful of the belief system that was already in place, as

opposed to being done by force or against the will of the

'believers.'

CONTENT

The articles I pulled for the purposes of this ethical

exploration came from the Ohiolink database and the

Ecopsychology Journal when I searched "Christian

missionary ethics." The articles that are included seemed

to touch on the topic of the ethics of Christian missionary

work and/or possible relevance to field work in a foreign

land, which I could find useful as I consider working in the wilderness with people of different backgrounds, traveling to different countries, and exploring different cultures in pursuit of my own ecopsychological practice.

JUDGING OTHERS

In *Judging Others*, Aaron Stalnaker (2008) looked at the *History, Ethics, and the Purposes of Comparison*. What this article helped me to realize is that "one compares things of the same sort in order to judge which of them is superior, which inferior," so that if a missionary goes into a land and compares the prevailing belief system with their own, therein could lie the beginning of a problem in behavior or treatment (p. 425). If a missionary (or an ecopsychologist doing field work) recognizes that "comparisons are always intellectual maneuvers undertaken for some human purpose, not just for the sake of pure knowledge," then they can acknowledge their true purpose and at least work to correct or account for that factor in their work (p. 431). I can say that I have the goal of pure knowledge when I talk to someone about the healing properties of nature, but it is my hope that they will engage in a relationship with the natural world in a loving and sustainable way. If that does not happen, then how would I react? Is it enough – can it be enough – that I tell them the 'good news' of the effects of such a relationship so that they are informed when they make their choices about how to treat the Earth?

What makes the situation difficult is that you do need to have a way to determine if you are successful, and another person converting to your belief system – to Christianity – can be one way to account for your work. My hope is that I can find a way to convert someone, have them adopt my ideals – or environmentally sustainable behavior – by first attempting to understand their point of view or respecting that it may be different. If we are clear about boundaries, about the central belief system, practices of the person or the culture we are engaged with, we are better able to see that culture – or a person in a certain culture – as unified, as an integrated whole "rather than like the fraught human collectivities we experience every day," as if it – or they – "exist in a vacuum" (p. 434). It is important to look at the whole because "social context does matter to moral evaluation, even if it does not insulate or isolate one person...or one group from others" (p. 435).

While I agree that it is likely not possible for a person to be nonjudgmental, I appreciate the idea that we must understand a person and their culture because "we cannot help but make recourse both to our developing sense of what was or is justifiable in their context" (p. 437). It is also important to note the ways in which judgment can be a problem so that it can be identified and addressed. Stalnaker notes that the more obvious problems that can result from judgment are "ignorance, incomprehension, misperception, or even misinformation," while more subtle problems that could arise include things like misconceptions and a loss of objectivity (p. 439).

NATURE ETHICS

Although I had some reservations about including

the *Review of Nature Ethics by Marti Kheel, as* written by

Grace G. Campbell (2010), because it is an article about

another work, I was also curious about the insights I would

receive about *Nature Ethics* through the critical analysis of

another reader. What I did come to find was an

introduction to the idea that traditional environmental

ethics were masculine in nature and this book – *Nature*

Ethics – "lays the groundwork for a new ecofeminist

framework" that is inclusive and compassionate as well as

ecological in its sense of values (p. 195). What this

thought does is not only remind me to consider the

principles of ecopsychology when evaluating my work, but

that the problem with the current human-nature

relationship is that it is masculine in nature – similar to the

impression I have been exploring of Christian missionary

work. Although "ecofeminism refers to a "loosely-knit

philosophical and practical orientation linking the

concerns of women to the larger natural world," I am

defining masculine in nature as a dominating position that can be seen as threatening or superior and judgmental (p. 196).

What I find an interesting point to consider in ethics and the dominant/submissive context is the language used; by language I am thinking about naming in particular. Because of how I was introduced to the land, I know the landmark in the red centre of Australia by its aboriginal name – Uluru – rather than by its European name – Ayers Rock. Although I call the large landmass that is visible from Lake Washington, Mount Rainier I was shocked to find it had its own indigenous name – Talal, Tahoma, or Tacoma – and the information opened up another layer of history I would not have considered otherwise. For this reason – to open up another level of discussion – Campbell notes that Kheel consciously chooses "to use other-than-human animals to remind [us] that humans are also animals and to stress kinship ties" so that we can get at the "deeper psychological roots in masculine identity" and open up to a concern for "other-than-human animals" (pp. 195-196).

What is also interesting about the use of language is that I would understand if the use of masculine and eco-feminine terminology would offend some people – especially those who strongly identify with their gender or have a heightened sensitivity to blame. My first thought regarding the use of language, is that those in masculine positions (Christian missionaries or people) should be or feel compelled to protect those in the feminine positions (indigenous populations or Earth) (p. 196). With this article I am able to see a connection between an ecopsychologist and Christian missionary because, just as Some' found the actions of the missionaries to be hypocritical to the scripture he read, some could find an ecopsychologist – or ecofeminist – also hypocritical if they give homes to domestic other-than-human animals while "advocating a world in which other animals no longer live in captivity" (p. 197).

MISSION AND HUMAN IDENTITY

I chose to include *Mission and Human Identity* by Brian Stanley (2009) because I suspected topics that are tied to how a person identifies him or herself – like their relationship with the divine – would present interesting insights into ethical behavior. The fact that the article focuses in on *the Light of Edinburgh 1910,* is a subtext that I believe makes sense because it would be a chance for me to gain insight into missionary work on a massive scale. In fact, the first potential for conflict that I notice Stanley point out is that "Christianity affirms that the good news of Jesus Christ is the key to human reconciliation," which immediately has me thinking that even the best of intentions – helping another person to become reconciled – has the potential to be harmful or at least insight a power struggle as it is established that Jesus Christ – the crux of Christianity – is the key (p. 81). Even with the idea that "the best hope for reconciling warring humanity with itself appears to lie in the propagation of the gospel of Christ," use of the word "propagation" in conjunction with "the gospel of Christ" not only puts the mission in a superior position, or a position of judgment, but also brings up images – for me – brainwashing or bombarding a group with a message until they "relinquish their position and fall into submission" (p. 81).

Because of the thought that "human identity is only made complete by the restoration of the image of God," there is an opportunity for conflict since those who judge sin to be present insist that the reconciliation – the joining of the Christian church – must occur for the situation to be rectified (p. 81). An opportunity for conflict is also present because the background of the missionaries at this time considered those not baptized to be less than human which – if not accounted for – could also result in inhumane treatment of others (p. 87). According to Stanley, "western Christian presentations of the gospel in India have been...marked by attitudes of superiority and aggression...[because]...to assert the sole Lordship of Jesus Christ over all peoples" is a kind of "theological oppression of the South by the North" (p. 86). Stanley also reports that "there are many people in North America and Europe who believe that those in the South are poor because they follow religions other than Christianity," and in Asian minds, Christianity is associated with the West and "its history of colonial aggression...[so]...the call to conversion to Christ poses major problems of justice and identity" (p. 86). These ideas not only open me up to global perceptions on the topic, but also national history as I found out – for what I believe to be the first time – that even the Christopher Columbus voyage in 1492 was an attempt at "reclamation of Spain for the Christian faith" (p. 88). This helps me to understand why Native Americans – and later Africans – were relegated to less than human status (p. 89).

What Stanley manages to do is proceed to help me recognize where ethical standards would come in, and that is in finding "a way of living with and acknowledging the integrity of those who are not of our faith." This is an important point when you consider that Christian

missionaries are talking about the gospel of Jesus and

Jesus was Jewish (p. 82). In order to acknowledge the

integrity of others Stanley seems to suggest that "religious

believers...repudiate the idea that religious truths are

universal timeless ideal forms to be taught to all peoples in

all ages" (p. 83). It is in the idea of a universal truth that

the opportunity for judgment finds a foothold because "if

all truth...is the same for everyone at all times, then if I am

right, you are wrong. If I care about truth I must convert

you to my point of view, and if you refuse to be converted,

beware" (p. 83). This use of language by Stanley suggests

to me that ethics is a code of conduct because "Jewish

faith...believes in one God but not in one religion culture,

or truth" – which suggests being respectful of those with

another faith especially when if you consider the "covenant

with Israel, to be a holy or "different" people" was given as

a way to "teach humanity the dignity of difference" (p. 83).

This leads me to understand that the ethics of Christian

missionary work lays not "in the proclamation of a

distinctively Christian gospel, but rather in 'co-operation with neighbors of other faiths for common purposes in society'" (p. 87).

It is in these moments that I also realize – not just the importance of language and naming – but of finding out the true and evolving definition of words because in knowing that the goal for Christian missionaries is to reconcile people to Christ, finding out that reconciliation is normally translated as "*katallagē* (which has a precise meaning of 'exchange'")) suggests that reconciliation is about coming to Christ "without surrendering our identity" (p. 92). If in fact the true mission or "commission" is to "bring the *ethne*, human beings in all the rich diversity...into a process of learning together to obey everything that Jesus has commanded us," then the ethical principles of Christian missionary work would seem to be "to teach others, in all their diverse particularity, to be learners alongside us" (p. 94).

ETHICS AND THE ENGINEER

In sifting through *Ethics and the Engineer* by W. Richard Bowen (2010), my interest was in combining ethics in a profession with a theological approach. Bowen points out that the commandments to love God and neighbor combine intention and values with understanding responsibility as being "'accountable *for* and accountable *to*' and nurturing 'a positive sense of vocation or calling'" (pp. 229-230). For Bowen this meant "more attention should be given to responsible creativity" by the engineer so that the priority is "serving life and society'" (p. 230). In the case of the ecopsychologist, making it a priority to serve life and society would be responsible practice in putting life and society in service to each other so that the Earth and the Human are on equal footing.

When Bowen considers that the focus is on "technical ingenuity" instead of on "helping people" I am reminded that Theodore Roszak (1998) called for ecopsychology to be "postindustrial not anti-industrial" so that the sanity of urban-industrial culture can be called into question without the rejection of the "technological genius of our species or some life-enhancing measure of the industrial power we have assembled" (p. 7). Bowen (2010) went on to bring in the language of "I" which recognizes that "the world of I-IT is that of experiencing and using;" while I-You sees the "uniqueness and integrity of the person encountered but acknowledges that the interaction may be brief and lacking in intimacy;" and I-Thou is "only saying what a candid reader might find in the primitive message of the New Testament, especially in the teaching of Jesus" (pp. 231, 232, 235). I am – in this moment – mindful that the aim of my practice, of ecopsychology, is to have people consider the natural world as an experience with the aim of sustaining and equipping human life, but not in a way that objectifies nature as being in service to the human animal for a treatment protocol rather than a living, breathing being in its own right. As Bowen says "we need to hear the voice of others saying, 'It's me here, please help me,'" which

reminds me that the book that called ecopsychology by

name is *The Voice of the Earth* (p. 232). Just as Bowen

suggests the engineer should respond by saying "here I am

for the others," the ecopsychologist must remind the

human animal that we are to have the same response

when we hear the Earth call for help (p. 232). Bowen sees

an example of the cry for help as the story of the Good

Samaritan from the Bible – which suggests that ethical

behavior means giving priority to the poor, where poor

denotes the biblical sense of those 'dominated, oppressed,

humiliated, instrumentalized,'" (p. 239). Bowen also

points out that the parable of the Good Samaritan has been

seen as an example of the Christian approach to ethics

because it focuses in on the "face-to-face, person-to-person

compassionate action beyond the bounds of immediate

community" (p. 242)

Bowen reminds me – as I liken ecopsychologists to

engineers – that "the radical principle of Christian ethics is

the face-to-face of the person-to-person relationship in the concrete, real, satisfied, happy, *community,*" and there is "no higher assessment of the value of a human person than that provided by an analogy based on divine personhood" (pp. 239, 241). Divine personhood "provides a fundamental basis for prioritizing persons before technical ingenuity" (p. 241). In considering divine personhood the ecopsychologist, like "the professional engineer who is a Christian will be part of at least three social groupings: a society, a practice and a Church" and we will not only recognize that "no person can live in the modern world without being part of the broader society, local, national or transnational" we can help convey that to the masses that the human animal cannot live without being part of the broader natural world (p. 242). It would then seem to me that ethical principles, in light of Christian theology and the world of the engineer, should strive to recognize "the benefit of its participants" as well as "concern for others" (p. 242).

PROTESTANT ETHICS

In looking at the *Protestant Ethics among Chinese Missionaries* by Laruen Pfister (2005), I had hoped to gain further insights into the kind of ethical behavior in which I should or should not be engaged especially in light of the association of Western culture with colonial aggression and Christianity. In fact I am introduced to the idea of "religious colonization" which came up "within Chinese spheres of Protestant missionary activity" (p. 96). What I found interesting about this article was that an "accommodating missiological position" as well as an appreciation for the indigenous cultures, was not only seen as an "unusual approach to Christian mission work," but led to what I would call the opposite effect of Christian conversion: rejection of the "Lutheran form of orthopraxy and adopt something more sectarian in nature" (p. 97). An ethical dilemma then arises where "the more [the Christian missionaries] articulated their positions to Chinese persons, the more they potentially or actually risked opposition" (p. 98).

In an "indirect" and "less confrontational form of missionary education" religious classes were not required to be taken even though they were offered, converts were not baptized, and Christian literature was provided for students with its consumption being left to each individual person" (p. 103). This gives me the example of choice in the process of conversion that I had been looking for. The example provided in this article seemed to suggest that the measure of success was not the fact of conversion to Christianity, so much as it was – inspired by the impressions of Jesus – "the greatness of the tasks one achieves rather than the words one speaks" (p. 106). The purpose then becomes a means of helping to produce "a 'new humanness' or 'new humanity' (*Neue Menschheit*) which transcended the cultural limitations and civilizational biases of both European and Chinese worldviews" (p. 107). These kinds of "cross-cultural religious synthesis" – which included non-confrontational missiological strategies and "creative...alternatives to new

Chinese Protestant religious forms of life" – were the result

of the sociological influences of "modern Protestant

missionary activities in China"

(pp. 110-111).

SCOTTISH MISSIONARIES

Scottish Missionaries and African Healers by

Markku Hokkanen (2004) not only showed promise in

exposing me to the ethics of Christian missionary work,

but offered a unique opportunity to look at it in the context

of indigenous wisdom that was inclusive of the African

population and the topic of shamanism. Immediately what

I find interesting is the academic value of the missionary

experience because "missionaries often spent more time in

Africa than most anthropologists, sometimes their entire

lives, sharing their everyday life with Africans and

acquiring a remarkable fluency in the vernacular

languages" (p. 321). In fact, "to a historian, these

narratives not only provide sources for studying the

missionary thought and language, but also offer valuable

clues and new insights to...'the colonial situation,' a

complex period of interaction requiring continuing interpretation" (p. 343). Hokkanen points out that the underlying difference between the missionary and the anthropologist is "the intellectual particularity of their respective purposes" (p. 321). What also makes this article a unique addition is that the reference point is the medical missionary, which meant "demonstrating the superiority of Western medicine to the medical traditions of other religions" was the tactic employed in order to "attack indigenous 'priest-physicians'" as a means of preparing the way for an eventual "religious conversion" (p. 322). In fact, "any public recognition of African medical skills would have questioned the value of medical mission at a time when one quarter of European missionaries died from illness and could have endangered the public support of the mission." (p. 341)

In order to attack priest-physicians, the medical missionaries claimed that indigenous medicine was "based on superstition, ignorance, false religious beliefs and lack of scientific knowledge" while hypocritically suggesting that "'native' medicine could be a source of new, effective drugs" (p. 322). I am reminded of the I-It relationship of finding the usefulness of the finished product but not the knowledge that generated it. Not only was there little attempt to understand the culture of indigenous medicine because it was assumed to be flawed, but the connection was then made to indigenous religion while there was a "strong rejection and derision" among the "Western observers were Christian medical missionaries" (p. 322). This reaction to the priest-physicians were based on perceptions that some of the "'native doctors' had considerable power based on deceit" by "playing on the fears and supernatural beliefs of their patients;" this despite some of them being "skillful in assessing when a sickness was severe" (p. 324).

The difference between the missionary and the anthropologist is notable when you consider that missionary publications paid more attention to the narrative of the "medical missionary, armed with the light of the Gospel and medical science" overcomes challenges

and a 'native doctor' that is abusing his people (p. 325).

Even the use of terms such as 'witch-doctor,' paints the

picture of a "medical mission triumphing over the African

doctors" as well as tackling the "belief in ancestral spirits

and in witchcraft" (p. 327). As the missionary views

matched that of Britain at the time, it makes it clearer to

me that ethical principles should account for the culture of

the missionary as well as the culture where the mission

work is being carried out in order to account for what

might influence the work being done.

ETHICAL ISSUES AND GUIDELINES

It was at this point in my exploration that I realized

I had some good ideas but I did not have a clear or succinct

idea of what ethics are and what ethical standards should

be in the practice of psychology, let alone ecopsychology.

In order to have a succinct set of guidelines for my

behavior I looked at *Ethical Issues and Guidelines in*

Psychology by Philip Banyard and Cara Flanagan (2005).

Come to find out, "ethics are the rules and guidelines that we use to make judgments of right and wrong," which would be not unlike the code of conduct I have been considering (p. 2). Although I had seen reference to morals or moral principles in the previous ethics article, Banyard and Flanagan explain that "morals, which are rules to guide our behavior...are based on a number of socially agreed principles," while "ethics are a moral framework that is applied to a narrow group of people" which can be broken down into four categories: "consequences, actions, character and motive" (pp. 26, 27). Now in my case the narrow group of people would be ecopsychologists who, according to Banyard and Flanagan, should engage in practices like debriefing participants who participate in their exercises because it "gives the researcher [or ecopsychologist] an opportunity to assess the effects of the research procedures and offer some form of counseling if necessary" (p. 61). This makes sense to me when I consider that revelations attributed to Joanna Macy include working through our grief for the ailing Earth that either 'suddenly comes to our attention' or is a 'throbbing sensation that is always there' (Macy, 2008, p. 2). Something else ecopsychologists should do when working with people is make it clear that the person does not have to participate so that "if the participant does feel harmed or undermined in any way, he or she can quit" (p. 62).

Banyard and Flanagan also note that three ethical issues – consent, harm, privacy – all have to do with the rights of the participant (p. 92). The participant, in terms of these rights, can be an entire community in the case of socially sensitive research, "in which there are potential consequences or implications, either directly for the participants in the research of for the class of individuals represented by the research'" (p. 107). An example of research that impacts a community – as I have just realized when considering the topic of this paper – could be research done involving Christian missionaries as it would imply that they all behave according to the inference of the research. One way to account for the community would be to include them to be a part of the research process, and review of the final report (p. 117).

Ethics are also important to ecopsychologists because while they do not want to promote healing through a connection to the natural world, it is important to recognize that therapists need business, so critical system analysis is needed so that the therapist is not just agreeing with a common diagnosis of illness when it could be the system that is "turning as many of us as possible into 'victims' prepared to pay for therapy" (p. 135). I think part of the process of establishing my own code of ethics to live and work by would be in asking the same questions it is suggested researchers ask when they consider doing research with animals: To what extent is this valuable? To what extent is this acceptable or ethical? (p. 147). The premise here is that "the use of animals in medical research may be easier to justify than their use in psychological research" because it is easier to become emotional about certain issues and animals than others, while "a third consideration is context [because]…what might appear unethical here and now might seem perfectly acceptable in a different environment" (p. 147).   In the end, the point of these ethical issues is what I was looking for in the missionary/convert relationship: "a concern about sensitivity" that includes a recognition that these issues or topics are "considered private, stressful, or sacred...might cause stigmatization or fear;" as well as the potential for controversy or social conflict (p. 107). Cultural sensitivity would mean, similar to the indirect and non-confrontational missionary approach, "the understanding that enables us to gain access to individuals in society, to learn about their lifestyles and to communicate in ways that the individuals understand, believe, regard as relevant to themselves and are likely to act upon" (p. 110). The goal would then be to honor the world of the participant without imposing another will by attempting to reform a "people whose culture they would like to eradicate, or perhaps simply out of ignorance about the subjects' reality" (p. 110). These are all important considerations in light of the fact that psychologists "make contributions to the media, they have personal interactions with clients which are guided by a code of conduct and they develop theories and techniques that have a direct effect on the public" (p. 131).

Discussion/Summary

Because I recognize that "complexity makes the judgments harder," this paper is not meant to judge the ethical behavior of the subjects of each of the included articles; this paper is meant as an exploration of the ethical considerations I should engage in when I go out into the world to talk about the principles of ecopsychology (Stalnaker, 2008, p. 425). I also recognize that I am a member of a "species of critical reflection [so that] studying ethics requires us at the very least to pick relevant data to examine," and make "judgments of relevance and importance" (p. 430).

What I have chosen to do with this paper was to explore various cases to see what ethical considerations emerged. Without looking at actual ethical standards or the definition of ethics I came to realize that ethics were a code of conduct. The code of conduct I saw emerging as a result of my initial readings on Christian missionary work included: consulting the principles of ecopsychology in order to determine whether my work is ecopsychological in nature; treating each person in such a way so as to be respectful of their divine personhood – including giving them the freedom to be different, to make informed decisions, and to not be in a submissive role; acknowledging and controlling for times when I am judgmental; critically assessing the motives of the mission, the people involved with the mission; and preparing for the mission by giving considerations to the history, culture, role, and religion of the people involved.

What the introduction of the formal text helped me to do was clarify that ethics are about what is right and what is wrong in such a way that the participant and the community are protected. I am reminded in a personal conversation that medical personnel have the same idea when they are asked to treat people and if they cannot treat them, then they are to do no harm. What I found to be similar between the code of conduct I saw emerging from Christian missionary work and the ethical standards in psychology, was a focus on the freedom of choice. What I also realized during this process was that I did not account for how this work would stigmatize the missionary community. This has, as a result, helped me to see how easy it is to believe you are on the side of what is right in the name of protection for others.

REFERENCES

(2010). (Dictionary.com, LLC) Retrieved October 29, 2010, from Dictionary.com: http://dictionary.reference.com/

Banyard, P., & Flanagan, C. (2005). *Ethical issues and guidelines in psychology.* New York, NY: Routledge Taylor & Francis Group.

Bowen, W. R. (2010). Ethics and the engineer: Developing the basis of a theological approach. *Studies in Christian Ethics , 23* (3), pp. 227-248.

Brody, H. (2000). *The other side of eden: Hunters, farmers, and the shaping of the world.* New York City, NY: North Point Press.

Campbell, G. G. (2010, September). Review of Nature Ethics byMarti Kheel. *Ecopsychology , 2* (3), pp. 195-198.

Harper, D. (2001, November). Retrieved January 24, 2010, from Online etymology dictionary: http://www.etymonline.com/

Hokkanen, M. (2004). Scottish missionaries and African healers: Perceptions and relations in the Livingstonia Mission, 1875-1930. *Journal of Religion in Africa , 34* (3), pp. 320-347.

Macy, J. (2008, February 1). *The greatest danger.* Retrieved November 1, 2009, from Yes magazine: http://yesmagazine.org/issues/climate-solutions/the-greatest-danger

Pfister, L. (2005). Protestant ethics among Chinese missionaries, problems of indigenization, and the spirit of academic professionalization. *Journal of Classical Sociology , 5* (1), pp. 93-114.

Roszak, T. (1998). *Ecopsychology: Eight principles.* Retrieved January 11, 2010, from Ecopsychology on-line: Introducing ecopsychology:

http://ecopsychology.athabascau.ca/Final/intro.ht
m

Some', M. P. (1994). *Of water and the spirit: Ritual, magic, and initiation in the life of an African shaman.* New York, NY: Penguin Compass.

Stalnaker, A. (2008). Judging others; History, ethics, and the purposes of comparison. *The Journal of Religious Ethics, Inc.*, *36* (3), pp. 425-444.

Stanley, B. (2009). Mission and human identity in the light of Edinburgh 1910. *Mission Studies*, *26*, pp. 80-97.

Appendix B:

Ethics for Ecology

Code of Ethics

Preamble: This code provides guiding principles of conduct for all members of the Ecological Society of America and all ecologists certified by the Society. It is the desire and purpose of the Society to support and encourage ecological research and education, and to facilitate the application of ecological science in the management of ecological systems. Towards these ends, this Code is intended to further ecological understanding through the open and honest communication of research; to assure appropriate accessibility of accurate and reliable ecological information to employers, policy makers, and the public; and to encourage effective education and training in the disciplines of ecological science. Individuals aware of breaches of this Code are encouraged to refer to the Society's procedures for addressing violations of the Code, and to communicate with the Society's Executive Director who will explain the code and process.

General: All members of the Ecological Society of America and all ecologists certified by the Society should observe the following principles in the conduct of their professional affairs

a. Ecologists will offer professional advice and guidance only on those subjects in which they are informed and qualified through professional training or experience. They will strive to accurately represent ecological understanding and knowledge and to avoid and discourage dissemination of erroneous, biased, or exaggerated statements about ecology.

b. Ecologists will not represent themselves as spokespersons for the Society without express authorization by the President of ESA.

c. Ecologists will cooperate with other researchers whenever possible and appropriate to assure rapid interchange and dissemination of ecological knowledge.

d. Ecologists will not plagiarize in verbal or written communication, but will give full and proper credit to the works and ideas of others, and make every effort to avoid misrepresentation.

e. Ecologists will not fabricate, falsify, or suppress results, deliberately misrepresent research findings, or otherwise commit scientific fraud.

f. Ecologists will conduct their research so as to avoid or minimize adverse environmental effects of their presence and activities, and in compliance with legal requirements for protection of researchers, human subjects, or research organisms and systems.

g. Ecologists will not discriminate against others, in the course of their work on the basis of gender, sexual orientation, marital status, creed, religion, race, color, national origin, age, economic status, disability, or organizational affiliation.

h. Ecologists will not practice or condone harassment in any form in any professional context.

i. In communications, ecologists should clearly differentiate facts, opinions, and hypotheses.

j. Ecologists will not seek employment, grants, or gain, nor attempt to injure the reputation or professional opportunities of another scientist by false, biased, or undocumented claims, by offers of gifts or favors, or by any other malicious action.

Certified Ecologists: Ecologists certified by the Ecological Society of America are expected to adhere to all sections of the Code; the following principles apply particularly to such individuals.

a. Certified ecologists will present evidence of their qualifications, including professional training, publications, and experience, when requested in connection with their work as a certified ecologist.

b. Certified ecologists will inform a prospective or current employer or client of any professional or personal interests which may impair the objectivity of their work, and, upon request, provide clients and employers with this Code.

c. Certified ecologists will respect requests for confidentiality from their employers or clients, provided that such confidentiality does not require violation of this Code or of legal statutes. Should conflicts arise between maintenance of confidentiality and legal or ethical standards, certified ecologists should advise clients or employers of the conflict in writing.

d. In seeking employment through bids, certified ecologists will describe salaries and fees and the extent and kinds of service to be rendered as accurately and fully as possible.

e. Certified ecologists should use resources available to them through institutional employment, in performance of work contracted independently of their employing institution, only with the full knowledge and consent of the employing institution. Inappropriate use of access to institutional resources should be avoided; the appropriateness of particular uses of institutional resources should be addressed by the employing institution.

f. Certified ecologists will accept compensation for a particular service or report from one source only, except with the full knowledge and consent of all concerned parties.

g. Certified ecologists will utilize, or recommend utilization of appropriate experts whenever such action is essential to solving a problem.

h. Certified ecologists will not knowingly associate professionally with, or allow the use of their names, reports, maps, or other technical materials by any enterprise known to be illegal or fraudulent.

i. Certified ecologists may advertise their services, but may not use misleading, false, or deceptive advertising. If Society certification is noted in advertisement, the level of certification must be included.

Publication: The following principles of ethical professional conduct apply to members reviewing, editing, or publishing grant proposals and papers in the professional literature in general, and particularly to all ecologists seeking publication in the Society's journals.

a. Researchers will claim authorship of a paper only if they have made a substantial contribution. Authorship may legitimately be claimed if researchers
   1. conceived the ideas or experimental design;
   2. participated actively in execution of the study;
   3. analyzed and interpreted the data; or
   4. wrote the manuscript.

b. Researchers will not add or delete authors from a manuscript submitted for publication without consent of those authors.

c. Researchers will not include as coauthor(s) any individual who has not agreed to the content of the final version of the manuscript.

d. Researchers will not submit for publication any manuscript containing data they are not authorized to use. ESA assumes the principal investigator(s) of a research project retain the right to control use of resulting unpublished data unless otherwise specified by contract or explicit agreement.

e. Researchers will not represent research results as new if they have been published or submitted elsewhere, or submit a manuscript for publication while it is under review for possible publication elsewhere.

f. Editors or reviewers will treat manuscripts under review as confidential, recognizing them as intellectual property of the author(s).

g. When using ideas or results of others in manuscripts submitted for publication, researchers will give full attribution of sources. If the ideas or results have not been published, they may not be used without permission of the original researcher. Illustrations or tables from other publications or manuscripts may be used only with permission of the copyright owner.

h. Ecologists will not serve as editors or reviewers of a manuscript if present or past connections with the author or the author's institution may prevent objective evaluation of the work.

i. Ecologists will not purposefully delay publication of another person's manuscript to gain advantage over that person.

j. Ecologists submitting manuscripts for publication will promptly report to editors any errors in research results or interpretations discovered after submission or publication.

Ecological Society of America
http://www.esa.org/aboutsa/codeethics.php
Accessed on December 22, 2012

APPENDIX C:

ETHICS FOR PSYCHOLOGY

The American Psychological Association's (APA) Ethical Principles of Psychologists and Code of Conduct (hereinafter referred to as the Ethics Code) consists of an Introduction, a Preamble, five General Principles and specific Ethical Standards...

Preamble

...This Ethics Code is intended to provide specific standards to cover most situations encountered by psychologists. It has as its goals the welfare and protection of the individuals and groups with whom psychologists work and the education of members, students and the public regarding ethical standards of the discipline...

General Principles

This section consists of General Principles. General Principles, as opposed to Ethical Standards, are aspirational in nature. Their intent is to guide and inspire psychologists toward the very highest ethical ideals of the profession. General Principles, in contrast to Ethical Standards, do not represent obligations and should not form the basis for imposing sanctions. Relying upon General Principles for either of these reasons distorts both their meaning and purpose.

Principle A: Beneficence and Nonmaleficence
Psychologists strive to benefit those with whom they work and take care to do no harm. In their professional actions,

psychologists seek to safeguard the welfare and rights of those with whom they interact professionally and other affected persons and the welfare of animal subjects of research. When conflicts occur among psychologists' obligations or concerns, they attempt to resolve these conflicts in a responsible fashion that avoids or minimizes harm. Because psychologists' scientific and professional judgments and actions may affect the lives of others, they are alert to and guard against personal, financial, social, organizational or political factors that might lead to misuse of their influence. Psychologists strive to be aware of the possible effect of their own physical and mental health on their ability to help those with whom they work.

Principle B: Fidelity and Responsibility
Psychologists establish relationships of trust with those with whom they work. They are aware of their professional and scientific responsibilities to society and to the specific communities in which they work. Psychologists uphold professional standards of conduct, clarify their professional roles and obligations, accept appropriate responsibility for their behavior and seek to manage conflicts of interest that could lead to exploitation or harm. Psychologists consult with, refer to, or cooperate with other professionals and institutions to the extent needed to serve the best interests of those with whom they work. They are concerned about the ethical compliance of their colleagues' scientific and professional conduct. Psychologists strive to contribute a portion of their professional time for little or no compensation or personal advantage.

Principle C: Integrity

Psychologists seek to promote accuracy, honesty and truthfulness in the science, teaching and practice of psychology. In these activities psychologists do not steal, cheat or engage in fraud, subterfuge or intentional misrepresentation of fact. Psychologists strive to keep their promises and to avoid unwise or unclear commitments. In situations in which deception may be ethically justifiable to maximize benefits and minimize harm, psychologists have a serious obligation to consider the need for, the possible consequences of, and their responsibility to correct any resulting mistrust or other harmful effects that arise from the use of such techniques.

Principle D: Justice

Psychologists recognize that fairness and justice entitle all persons to access to and benefit from the contributions of psychology and to equal quality in the processes, procedures and services being conducted by psychologists. Psychologists exercise reasonable judgment and take precautions to ensure that their potential biases, the boundaries of their competence and the limitations of their expertise do not lead to or condone unjust practices.

Principle E: Respect for People's Rights and Dignity

Psychologists respect the dignity and worth of all people, and the rights of individuals to privacy, confidentiality, and self-determination. Psychologists are aware that special safeguards may be necessary to protect the rights and welfare of persons or communities whose vulnerabilities impair autonomous decision making. Psychologists are aware of and respect cultural, individual and role differences, including those based on age, gender, gender identity, race, ethnicity, culture, national origin, religion, sexual orientation, disability, language and socioeconomic status and consider these factors when working with members of such groups. Psychologists try to eliminate the effect on their work of biases based on those factors, and they do not knowingly participate in or condone activities of others based upon such prejudices.

Standards

1. Resolving Ethical Issues
2. Competence
3. Human Relations
4. Privacy and Confidentiality
5. Advertising and Other Public Statements
6. Record Keeping and Fees
7. Education and Training
8. Research and Publication
9. Assessment
10. Therapy

Humane Care and Use of Animals in Research

(a) Psychologists acquire, care for, use, and dispose of animals in compliance with current federal, state and local laws and regulations, and with professional standards.

(b) Psychologists trained in research methods and experienced in the care of laboratory animals supervise all procedures involving animals and are responsible for ensuring appropriate consideration of their comfort, health and humane treatment.

(c) Psychologists ensure that all individuals under their supervision who are using animals have received instruction in research methods and in the care, maintenance and handling of the species being used, to the extent appropriate to their role. (See also Standard 2.05, Delegation of Work to Others.)

(d) Psychologists make reasonable efforts to minimize the discomfort, infection, illness and pain of animal subjects.

(e) Psychologists use a procedure subjecting animals to pain, stress or privation only when an alternative procedure is unavailable and the goal is justified by its prospective scientific, educational or applied value.

(f) Psychologists perform surgical procedures under appropriate anesthesia and follow techniques to avoid infection and minimize pain during and after surgery.

(g) When it is appropriate that an animal's life be terminated, psychologists proceed rapidly, with an effort to minimize pain and in accordance with accepted procedures.

American Psychological Association

http://www.apa.org/ethics/code/index.aspx?item=1
Accessed December 22, 2012 & February 20, 2013

Appendix D:

Ethics for Environmentalism

The objectives of Environmental Professionals are to
conduct their personal and professional lives and activities
in an ethical manner. Honesty, justice and courtesy form
moral philosophy which, associated with a mutual interest
among people, constitute the foundation of
ethics. Environmental Professionals should recognize such
a standard, not in passive observance, but as a set of
dynamic principles guiding their conduct and way of
life. It is their duty to practice their profession according
to this Code of Ethics.

As the keystone of professional conduct is integrity,
Environmental Professionals will discharge their duties
with fidelity to the public, their employers, clients, with
fairness and impartiality to all. It is their duty to interest
themselves in public welfare, and to be ready to apply
their special knowledge for the benefit of mankind and
their environment.

Creed

The objectives of an Environmental Professional are:

1. To recognize and attempt to reconcile societal and
individual human needs with responsibility for physical,
natural, and cultural systems.

2. To promote and develop policies, plans, activities and projects that achieve complementary and mutual support between natural and man-made, and present and future components of the physical, natural and cultural environment.

Ethics

As an Environmental Professional I will:

1. Be personally responsible for the validity of all data collected, analyses performed, or plans developed by me or under my direction. I will be responsible and ethical in my professional activities.

2. Encourage research, planning, design, management and review of activities in a scientifically and technically objective manner. I will incorporate the best principles of the environmental sciences for the mitigation of environmental harm and enhancement of environmental quality.

3. Not condone misrepresentation of work I have performed or that was performed under my direction.

4. Examine all of my relationships or actions, which could be legitimately interpreted as a conflict of interest by clients, officials, the public or peers. In any instance where I have financial or personal interest in the activities with which they are directly or indirectly involved, I will make a full disclosure of that interest to my employer, client, or other affected parties.

5. Not engage in conduct involving dishonesty, fraud, deceit, or misrepresentation or discrimination.

6. Not accept fees wholly or partially contingent on the client€™s desired result where that desired result conflicts with my professional judgment.

Guidance for Practice as an
Environmental Professional

As an Environmental Professional I will:

1. Encourage environmental planning to begin in the earliest stages of project conceptualization.

2. Recognize that total environmental management involves the consideration of all environmental factors including: technical, economical, ecological, and sociopolitical and their relationships.

3. Incorporate the best principle of design and environmental planning when recommending measures to reduce environmental harm and enhance environmental quality.

4. Conduct my analysis, planning, design and review my activities primarily in subject areas for which I am qualified, and shall encourage and recognize that participation of other professionals in subject areas where I am less experienced. I shall utilize and participate in interdisciplinary teams wherever practical to determine impacts, define and evaluate all reasonable alternatives to proposed actions, and assess short-term versus long-term productivity with and without the project or action.

5. Seek common, adequate, and sound technical grounds for communication with and respect for the contributions of other professionals in developing and reviewing policies, plans, activities and projects.

6. Determine that the policies, plans, activities or projects in which I am involved are consistent with all governing laws, ordinances, guidelines, plans and policies to the best of my knowledge and ability.

7. Encourage public participation at the earliest feasible time in an open and productive atmosphere.

8. Conduct my professional activities in a manner that ensures consideration of technically and economically feasible alternatives.

Encourage Development of the Profession

As an Environmental Professional I will:

1. Assist in maintaining the integrity and competence of my profession.

2. Encourage education and research and the development of useful technical information relating to the environmental field.

3. Be prohibited from lobbying in the name of the National Association of Environmental Professionals.

4. Advertise and present my services in a manner that avoids the use of material and methods that may bring discredit to the profession.

National Association of Environmental Professionals
http://www.naep.org/code-of-ethics
Accessed 2 January 2013

APPENDIX E:

ECOPSYCHOLOGY 'FAMILY TREE'

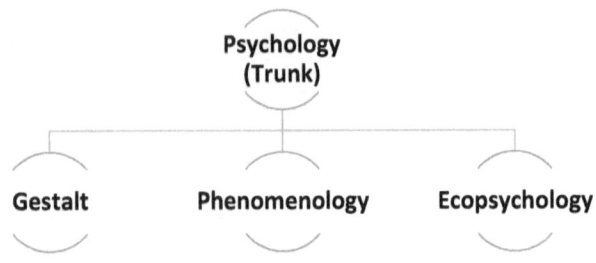

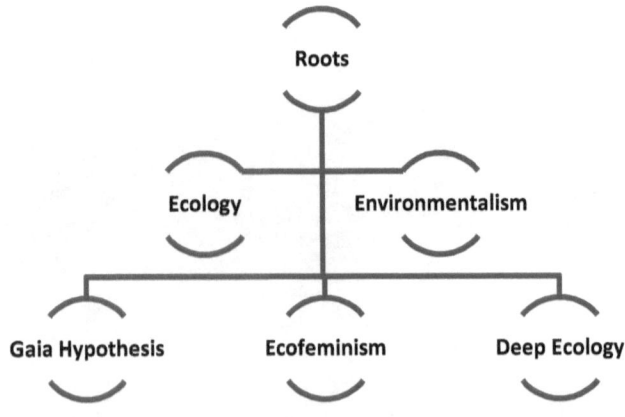

Appendix F:

The Ten Commandments

Exodus 20

King James Version

And God spake all these words, saying,

2 I am the LORD thy God, which have brought thee out of the land of Egypt, out of the house of bondage.

3 Thou shalt have no other gods before me.

4 Thou shalt not make unto thee any graven image, or any likeness of anything that is in heaven above, or that is in the earth beneath, or that is in the water under the earth.

5 Thou shalt not bow down thyself to them, nor serve them: for I the LORD thy God am a jealous God, visiting the iniquity of the fathers upon the children unto the third and fourth generation of them that hate me;

6 And shewing mercy unto thousands of them that love me, and keep my commandments.

7 Thou shalt not take the name of the LORD thy God in vain; for the LORD will not hold him guiltless that taketh his name in vain.

8 Remember the sabbath day, to keep it holy.

9 Six days shalt thou labour, and do all thy work:

10 But the seventh day is the sabbath of the LORD thy God: in it thou shalt not do any work, thou, nor thy son, nor thy daughter, thy manservant, nor thy maidservant, nor thy cattle, nor thy stranger that is within thy gates:

11 For in six days the LORD made heaven and earth, the sea, and all that in them is, and rested the seventh day: wherefore the LORD blessed the sabbath day, and hallowed it.

12 Honour thy father and thy mother: that thy days may be long upon the land which the LORD thy God giveth thee.

13 Thou shalt not kill.

14 Thou shalt not commit adultery.

15 Thou shalt not steal.

16 Thou shalt not bear false witness against thy neighbour.

17 Thou shalt not covet thy neighbour's house, thou shalt not covet thy neighbour's wife, nor his manservant, nor his maidservant, nor his ox, nor his ass, nor any thing that is thy neighbour's.

NEW INTERNATIONAL VERSION

And God spoke all these words:

2 "I am the LORD your God, who brought you out of Egypt, out of the land of slavery.

3 "You shall have no other gods before[a] me.

4 "You shall not make for yourself an image in the form of anything in heaven above or on the earth beneath or in the waters below. 5 You shall not bow down to them or

worship them; for I, the LORD your God, am a jealous God, punishing the children for the sin of the parents to the third and fourth generation of those who hate me, 6 but showing love to a thousand generations of those who love me and keep my commandments.

7 "You shall not misuse the name of the LORD your God, for the LORD will not hold anyone guiltless who misuses his name.

8 "Remember the Sabbath day by keeping it holy. 9 Six days you shall labor and do all your work, 10 but the seventh day is a sabbath to the LORD your God. On it you shall not do any work, neither you, nor your son or daughter, nor your male or female servant, nor your animals, nor any foreigner residing in your towns. 11 For in six days the LORD made the heavens and the earth, the sea, and all that is in them, but he rested on the seventh day. Therefore the LORD blessed the Sabbath day and made it holy.

12 "Honor your father and your mother, so that you may live long in the land the LORD your God is giving you.

13 "You shall not murder.

14 "You shall not commit adultery.

15 "You shall not steal.

16 "You shall not give false testimony against your neighbor.

17 "You shall not covet your neighbor's house. You shall not covet your neighbor's wife, or his male or female servant, his ox or donkey, or anything that belongs to your neighbor."

THE MESSAGE TRANSLATION

1-2 GOD spoke all these words:

I am GOD, your God,
  who brought you out of the land of Egypt,
  out of a life of slavery.

3 No other gods, only me.

4-6 No carved gods of any size, shape, or form of anything whatever, whether of things that fly or walk or swim. Don't bow down to them and don't serve them because *I* am GOD, your God, and I'm a most jealous God, punishing the children for any sins their parents pass on to them to the third, and yes, even to the fourth generation of those who hate me. But I'm unswervingly loyal to the thousands who love me and keep my commandments.

7 No using the name of GOD, your God, in curses or silly banter; GOD won't put up with the irreverent use of his name.

8-11 Observe the Sabbath day, to keep it holy. Work six days and do everything you need to do. But the seventh day is a Sabbath to GOD, your God. Don't do any work—not you, nor your son, nor your daughter, nor your servant, nor your maid, nor your animals, not even the foreign guest visiting in your town. For in six days GOD made Heaven, Earth, and sea, and everything in them; he rested on the seventh day. Therefore GOD blessed the Sabbath day; he set it apart as a holy day.

12 Honor your father and mother so that you'll live a long time in the land that God, your God, is giving you.

13 No murder.

14 No adultery.

[15] No stealing.

[16] No lies about your neighbor.

[17] No lusting after your neighbor's house—or wife or servant or maid or ox or donkey. Don't set your heart on anything that is your neighbor's.

BibleGateway.com
http://www.biblegateway.com/
Accessed 2 January 2013

APPENDIX G:

HIPPOCRATIC OATH

Hippocratic Oath: Classical Version

I swear by Apollo Physician and Asclepius and Hygieia and Panaceia and all the gods and goddesses, making them my witnesses, that I will fulfill according to my ability and judgment this oath and this covenant:

To hold him who has taught me this art as equal to my parents and to live my life in partnership with him, and if he is in need of money to give him a share of mine, and to regard his offspring as equal to my brothers in male lineage and to teach them this art—if they desire to learn it—without fee and covenant; to give a share of precepts and oral instruction and all the other learning to my sons and to the sons of him who has instructed me and to pupils who have signed the covenant and have taken an oath according to the medical law, but no one else.

I will apply dietetic measures for the benefit of the sick according to my ability and judgment; I will keep them from harm and injustice.

I will neither give a deadly drug to anybody who asked for it, nor will I make a suggestion to this effect. Similarly I will not give to a woman an abortive remedy. In purity and holiness I will guard my life and my art.

I will not use the knife, not even on sufferers from stone, but will withdraw in favor of such men as are engaged in this work.

Whatever houses I may visit, I will come for the benefit of the sick, remaining free of all intentional injustice, of all mischief and in particular of sexual relations with both female and male persons, be they free or slaves.

What I may see or hear in the course of the treatment or even outside of the treatment in regard to the life of men, which on no account one must spread abroad, I will keep to myself, holding such things shameful to be spoken about.

If I fulfill this oath and do not violate it, may it be granted to me to enjoy life and art, being honored with fame among all men for all time to come; if I transgress it and swear falsely, may the opposite of all this be my lot.

—Translation from the Greek by Ludwig Edelstein. From *The Hippocratic Oath: Text, Translation, and Interpretation*, by Ludwig Edelstein. Baltimore: Johns Hopkins Press, 1943.

Hippocratic Oath: Modern Version

I swear to fulfill, to the best of my ability and judgment, this covenant:

I will respect the hard-won scientific gains of those physicians in whose steps I walk, and gladly share such knowledge as is mine with those who are to follow.

I will apply, for the benefit of the sick, all measures [that] are required, avoiding those twin traps of overtreatment and therapeutic nihilism.

I will remember that there is art to medicine as well as science, and that warmth, sympathy, and understanding may outweigh the surgeon's knife or the chemist's drug.

I will not be ashamed to say "I know not," nor will I fail to call in my colleagues when the skills of another are needed for a patient's recovery.

I will respect the privacy of my patients, for their problems are not disclosed to me that the world may know. Most especially must I tread with care in matters of life and death. If it is given me to save a life, all thanks. But it may also be within my power to take a life; this awesome responsibility must be faced with great humbleness and awareness of my own frailty. Above all, I must not play at God.

I will remember that I do not treat a fever chart, a cancerous growth, but a sick human being, whose illness may affect the person's family and economic stability. My responsibility includes these related problems, if I am to care adequately for the sick.

I will prevent disease whenever I can, for prevention is preferable to cure.

I will remember that I remain a member of society, with special obligations to all my fellow human beings, those sound of mind and body as well as the infirm.

If I do not violate this oath, may I enjoy life and art, respected while I live and remembered with affection thereafter. May I always act so as to preserve the finest traditions of my calling and may I long experience the joy of healing those who seek my help.

—Written in 1964 by Louis Lasagna, Academic Dean of the School of Medicine at Tufts University, and used in many medical schools today.

PBS: The Hippocratic Oath Today
http://www.pbs.org/wgbh/nova/body/hippocratic-oath-today.html
Accessed 2 January 2013

APPENDIX H:

ETHICS FOR THE INTERNATIONAL

COACHING FEDERATION

Part One: Definition of Coaching

Section 1: Definitions

- **Coaching:** Coaching is partnering with clients in a thought-provoking and creative process that inspires them to maximize their personal and professional potential.
- **A professional coaching relationship:** A professional coaching relationship exists when coaching includes a business agreement or contract that defines the responsibilities of each party.
- **An ICF Professional Coach:** An ICF Professional Coach also agrees to practice the ICF Professional Core Competencies and pledges accountability to the ICF Code of Ethics.

In order to clarify roles in the coaching relationship, it is often necessary to distinguish between the client and the sponsor. In most cases, the client and sponsor are the same person and therefore jointly referred to as the client. For purposes of identification, however, the International Coach Federation defines these roles as follows:

- **Client:** The "client" is the person(s) being coached.
- **Sponsor:** The "sponsor" is the entity (including its representatives) paying for and/or arranging for coaching services to be provided.

In all cases, coaching engagement contracts or agreements should clearly establish the rights, roles, and responsibilities for both the client and sponsor if they are not the same persons.

Part Two: The ICF Standards of Ethical Conduct

Preamble: ICF Professional Coaches aspire to conduct themselves in a manner that reflects positively upon the coaching profession; are respectful of different approaches to coaching; and recognize that they are also bound by applicable laws and regulations.

Section 1: Professional Conduct At Large

As a coach:

1) I will not knowingly make any public statement that is untrue or misleading about what I offer as a coach, or make false claims in any written documents relating to the coaching profession or my credentials or the ICF.

2) I will accurately identify my coaching qualifications, expertise, experience, certifications and ICF Credentials.

3) I will recognize and honor the efforts and contributions of others and not misrepresent them as my own. I understand that violating this standard may leave me subject to legal remedy by a third party.

4) I will, at all times, strive to recognize personal issues that may impair, conflict, or interfere with my coaching performance or my professional coaching relationships. Whenever the facts and circumstances necessitate, I will

promptly seek professional assistance and determine the action to be taken, including whether it is appropriate to suspend or terminate my coaching relationship(s).

5) I will conduct myself in accordance with the ICF Code of Ethics in all coach training, coach mentoring, and coach supervisory activities.

6) I will conduct and report research with competence, honesty, and within recognized scientific standards and applicable subject guidelines. My research will be carried out with the necessary consent and approval of those involved, and with an approach that will protect participants from any potential harm. All research efforts will be performed in a manner that complies with all the applicable laws of the country in which the research is conducted.

7) I will maintain, store, and dispose of any records created during my coaching business in a manner that promotes confidentiality, security, and privacy, and complies with any applicable laws and agreements

8) I will use ICF member contact information (e-mail addresses, telephone numbers, etc.) only in the manner and to the extent authorized by the ICF.

Section 2: Conflicts of Interest

As a coach:

9) I will seek to avoid conflicts of interest and potential conflicts of interest and openly disclose any such conflicts. I will offer to remove myself when such a conflict arises.

10) I will disclose to my client and his or her sponsor all anticipated compensation from third parties that I may pay or receive for referrals of that client.

11) I will only barter for services, goods or other non-monetary remuneration when it will not impair the coaching relationship.

12) I will not knowingly take any personal, professional, or monetary advantage or benefit of the coach-client relationship, except by a form of compensation as agreed in the agreement or contract.

Section 3: Professional Conduct with Clients

As a coach:

13) I will not knowingly mislead or make false claims about what my client or sponsor will receive from the coaching process or from me as the coach.

14) I will not give my prospective clients or sponsors information or advice I know or believe to be misleading or false.

15) I will have clear agreements or contracts with my clients and sponsor(s). I will honor all agreements or contracts made in the context of professional coaching relationships.

16) I will carefully explain and strive to ensure that, prior to or at the initial meeting, my coaching client and sponsor(s) understand the nature of coaching, the nature and limits of confidentiality, financial arrangements, and any other terms of the coaching agreement or contract.

17) I will be responsible for setting clear, appropriate, and culturally sensitive boundaries that govern any physical contact I may have with my clients or sponsors.

18) I will not become sexually intimate with any of my current clients or sponsors.

19) I will respect the client's right to terminate the coaching relationship at any point during the process, subject to the provisions of the agreement or contract. I will be alert to indications that the client is no longer benefiting from our coaching relationship.

20) I will encourage the client or sponsor to make a change if I believe the client or sponsor would be better served by another coach or by another resource.
21) I will suggest my client seek the services of other professionals when deemed necessary or appropriate.

Section 4: Confidentiality/Privacy

As a coach:

22) I will maintain the strictest levels of confidentiality with all client and sponsor information. I will have a clear agreement or contract before releasing information to another person, unless required by law.

23) I will have a clear agreement upon how coaching information will be exchanged among coach, client, and sponsor.

24) When acting as a trainer of student coaches, I will clarify confidentiality policies with the students.

25) I will have associated coaches and other persons whom I manage in service of my clients and their sponsors in a paid or volunteer capacity make clear agreements or contracts to adhere to the ICF Code of Ethics Part 2, Section 4: Confidentiality/Privacy standards and the entire ICF Code of Ethics to the extent applicable.

Part Three: The ICF Pledge of Ethics

As an ICF Professional Coach, I acknowledge and agree to honor my ethical and legal obligations to my coaching clients and sponsors, colleagues, and to the public at large. I pledge to comply with the ICF Code of Ethics, and to practice these standards with those whom I coach.

If I breach this Pledge of Ethics or any part of the ICF Code of Ethics, I agree that the ICF in its sole discretion may hold me accountable for so doing. I further agree that my accountability to the ICF for any breach may include sanctions, such as loss of my ICF membership and/or my ICF Credentials.

ICF
http://coachfederation.org/about-icf/ethics/icf-code-of-ethics/
Accessed 2 January 2013

APPENDIX I:

ETHICS OF APPRENTICESHIP

I hold the earth to be sacred, inviolable, a living entity to whom I owe my very life and death. I respect, protect, and conserve her, leaving as little trace as possible of my sojourn, or passage through, the wilderness. I teach others to do the same.

I am well trained, experienced in the various aspects of my profession, having acquired the skills, credentials, and personal mastery of the true professional, seeking always the safety and well-being of those I serve, doing nothing to harm their physical, emotional, mental, and spiritual health.

I use pancultural or traditional forms, allegories, prototypes, teachings, and ceremonial ways that are appropriate to the life goals of the individuals I serve. I respect the unity in cultural diversity, honoring in the monomyth, humanity's common roots. I heed the inner voices of my own ancestral heritage, heeding also the wisdom of many races, cultures, and colors.

I construct and maintain safe prototypes within which individuals may mark the end of the life transitions or personal crises, providing a beneficial means by which they may incorporate their wilderness passage into a new life purpose or station.

I do not allow others to undertake any ordeal, test, or rite that I myself have not personally experienced.

I network, in good will, with others in my profession, and honor and respect our differences as well as our similarities.

Steven Foster and Meredith Little
The Roaring of the Sacred River p. 95-96

Appendix J:

Leave No Trace

The Leave No Trace Seven Principles

The Leave No Trace Seven Principles are also available for <u>various environments and activities</u>.

Plan Ahead and Prepare

- Know the regulations and special concerns for the area you'll visit.
- Prepare for extreme weather, hazards, and emergencies.
- Schedule your trip to avoid times of high use.
- Visit in small groups when possible. Consider splitting larger groups into smaller groups.
- Repackage food to minimize waste.
- Use a map and compass to eliminate the use of marking paint, rock cairns or flagging.

Travel and Camp on Durable Surfaces

- Durable surfaces include established trails and campsites, rock, gravel, dry grasses or snow.
- Protect riparian areas by camping at least 200 feet from lakes and streams.
- Good campsites are found, not made. Altering a site is not necessary.
  - In popular areas:
    - Concentrate use on existing trails and campsites.
    - Walk single file in the middle of the trail, even when wet or muddy.
    - Keep campsites small. Focus activity in areas where vegetation is absent.

- In pristine areas:
- Disperse use to prevent the creation of campsites and trails.
- Avoid places where impacts are just beginning.

Dispose of Waste Properly

- Pack it in, pack it out. Inspect your campsite and rest areas for trash or spilled foods. Pack out all trash, leftover food and litter.
- Deposit solid human waste in catholes dug 6 to 8 inches deep, at least 200 feet from water, camp and trails. Cover and disguise the cathole when finished.
- Pack out toilet paper and hygiene products.
- To wash yourself or your dishes, carry water 200 feet away from streams or lakes and use small amounts of biodegradable soap. Scatter strained dishwater.

Leave What You Find

- Preserve the past: examine, but do not touch cultural or historic structures and artifacts.
- Leave rocks, plants and other natural objects as you find them.
- Avoid introducing or transporting non-native species.
- Do not build structures, furniture, or dig trenches.

Minimize Campfire Impacts

- Campfires can cause lasting impacts to the backcountry. Use a lightweight stove for cooking and enjoy a candle lantern for light.
- Where fires are permitted, use established fire rings, fire pans, or mound fires.
- Keep fires small. Only use sticks from the ground that can be broken by hand.

- Burn all wood and coals to ash, put out campfires completely, then scatter cool ashes.

Respect Wildlife
- Observe wildlife from a distance. Do not follow or approach them.
- Never feed animals. Feeding wildlife damages their health, alters natural behaviors, and exposes them to predators and other dangers.
- Protect wildlife and your food by storing rations and trash securely.
- Control pets at all times, or leave them at home.
- Avoid wildlife during sensitive times: mating, nesting, raising young, or winter.

Be Considerate of Other Visitors
- Respect other visitors and protect the quality of their experience.
- Be courteous. Yield to other users on the trail.
- Step to the downhill side of the trail when encountering pack stock.
- Take breaks and camp away from trails and other visitors.
- Let nature's sounds prevail. Avoid loud voices and noises.

The member-driven Leave No Trace Center for Outdoor Ethics teaches people how to enjoy the outdoors responsibly. This copyrighted information has been reprinted with permission from the Leave No Trace Center for Outdoor Ethics: www.LNT.org?

Leave No Trace Center for Outdoor Ethics
http://lnt.org/learn/7-principles
Accessed 2 January 2013

About the Author

Tiffany A. Dedeaux was educated at the University of Nevada, Reno where she earned a Bachelor of Arts in Broadcast Journalism with a minor in Social Psychology. She spent 14 years building her career, mostly as a video editor, until she transitioned into digital news production training. Her newfound status as a software trainer afforded her the opportunity to travel throughout the United States and Australia, where she then heard the call to become a guide. To add depth to her journey she explored being a wilderness quest guide as she attended Antioch University Seattle, where she earned a Masters of Arts in Psychology. Her coursework focused on Ecopsychology and Cultural Transformation. After graduation she trained to become a life coach and started her own practice, _Sacred Time_, to bring together the principles of ecopsychology with the empowering partnership of coaching.

About the Book

This is a time for change in our lives, professions, and climate. We don't have to go through it alone.

Offering a means of navigation in the wilderness of change, *Ethics and the Earth Missionary* is a journey to define, explore, and outline what the ethical standards could be for the field of ecopsychology and all of us who are looking to become more intentional in our relationship with the rest of the earth.

Utilizing metaphors as guides, Tiffany A. Dedeaux, weaves insights into a journey that elevates our level of awareness and assists in establishing a foundation of understanding we can reference in our personal, professional, and academic lives.

More than a set of rules one must abide by, a code of conduct can be a way to ensure that life is recognized and protected so that together we can adapt to the environmental, spiritual, and social changes ahead.

Notes

[i] We must remember that the human-made climate forcing is not coming on just a bit faster than natural forcings of the past; on the contrary, it is a rapid powerful blow, an order of magnitude greater than any natural forcings that we are aware of (*Storms of my Grandchildren*, p. 274). While this is one quote, my statement is a summary of my reading from this book.

[ii] At the root of *transition* is "transit," a voyage from one place to another. As in any voyage, there is a departure, a disorienting time of travel and, finally, a destination...To be in transit is to be in the process of leaving one thing, without having fully left it, and at the same time entering something else, without being fully a part of it (*Working Identity*, p. 54). This is from the section *In the Middle*. See also p. 65 and the section on *Living the Contradictions*.

[iii] "We will respond to the threat of climate change, knowing that the failure to do so would betray our children and future generations. Some may still deny the overwhelming judgment of science, but none can avoid the devastating impact of raging fires, and crippling drought, and more powerful storms" (from Barack Obama's second inaugural address on 21 January 2012).

[iv] We can argue about the cause for the weather change, and we can argue if the cause was human behavior or a natural cycle of weather patterns, but you can't argue about the effect. You can argue why the water is coming over the bank, but the water's coming over the bank, and when the water comes over the bank, it floods the tunnels and the subway system. That is a fact...Let's

address that fact (from <u>Rachel Maddow's interview with Governor Andrew Cuomo</u> on November 1, 2012). What I referenced and this quote are all listed in the transcripts of the online version of the segment.

[v] Insight alone does not bring about behavior change. Other self-changers begin with change processes that are most effective in the action stage…without having first gained awareness and readiness in the early stages. They try to modify behavior without awareness. This echoes a common criticism of behaviorism: Overt action without insight is likely to lead to temporary change (*Changing for Good,* p. 59). See also p. 47.

[vi] I can hear all the voices of ancestors crying out…it's a painful thing to experience…they're going to rise up again and what other people recognize as a hurricane is going to wipe out a lot of what they see (*Rooted in Water,* p. 155). This is in the Appendix, where I put my notes from the media used in a documentary.

[vii] People who can tolerate the painful discrepancies of the between0identities period, which reflect underlying ambivalence about letting go of the old or embracing the new, end up in a better position to make informed choices (*Working Identity,* p. 65).

[viii] This is an example to demonstrate how this book is organized. Here are notes and comments that relate to the referenced material so that you can have context or background without inundating the main text.

[ix] Nothing has been more futile than our effort over the past few centuries to establish values and define sanity within a cultural context that finds no place for the sacred and views life as a marginal anomaly in the universe. The cosmology that gave us that picture of the human condition has now faded from the scene. The time is ripe for a new dialogue between scientific intellect and human need (*The Voice of the Earth,* p. 17).

[x] Discovery of the New World rekindled a traditional European belief that an earthly paradise lay somewhere to the west…But, instead of paradise, the early settlers encountered a "howling," "dismal," and "terrible" wilderness that stretched beyond the European imagination of what "wild" was…Once survival was assured, the harshness of life encouraged a backwoods conservatism in farming. The pioneers developed a virulent enmity toward the wilderness, using military metaphors to discuss the coming of civilization (*American Cultural Patterns,* p. 114).

[xi] In every culture, on every continent, natural beauty has been a primary resource for helping people through difficult times..Beauty was used to gain fresh perspective on the world—an essential nudge toward the kind of clarity that often eludes people in times of emotional pain. In the heart of the Middle Ages...the faithful were sinking into a kind of malaise...The trouble, [Thomas] Aquinas would later explain, was quite simple: people were suffering from acedia because they'd somehow lost their ability to be in touch with the beauty of the natural world around them (*Shouting at the Sky,* p. xiii-xiv).

[xii] Paul Shepard...was the first ecopsychologist, the first thinker in the environmental movement to apply psychological categories to our treatment of the planet (*The Voice of the Earth,* p. 327).

[xiii] Twigs and buds are the most helpful features to look for in the winter (*The Tree Identification Book,* p. 98).

[xiv] 1. The core of the mind is the ecological unconscious...2. The contents of the ecological unconscious represent, in some degree, at some level of mentality, the living record of cosmic evolution, tracing back to distant initial conditions in the history of time...3...The goal of ecopsychology is to awaken the inherent sense of environmental reciprocity that lies within the ecological unconscious...4...Ecopsychology seeks to recover the child's innately animistic quality of experience in functionally "sane" adults...5. The ecological ego matures toward a sense of ethical responsibility with the planet that is as vividly experienced as our ethical responsibility to other people...6...Among the therapeutic projects most important to ecopsychology is the re-evaluation of certain compulsively "masculine" character traits that permeate our structures of political power and which drive us to dominate nature as if it were an alien and rightless realm...7...Ecopsychology...deeply questions the essential sanity of our gargantuan urban-industrial culture, whether capitalistic or collectivistic in its organization...8. Ecopsychology holds that the interplay between planetary and personal well-being (*The Voice of the Earth, pgs. 320-321*).

[xv] Ecofeminists bring attention to the historical fact that under patriarchal rule the repressing and exploiting of women has gone hand-in-hand with the repressing and exploiting of the natural world. The domination of nature, say ecofeminists,

cannot be satisfactorily understood unless viewed as a feminist issue (*Radical Ecopsychology*, p. 19).

xvi The Earth speaks to us through our bodies and psyches. She often cries, and many of us feel her tears and see her pain. Recognizing her voice is perception (*The Skill of Ecological Perception* section of *Ecopsychology: Restoring the Earth; Healing the Mind*, p. 214).

xvii "Ecopsychology" is the name most often used for this emerging synthesis of the psychological (here intended to embrace the psychotherapeutic and the psychiatric) and the ecological. Several other terms have been suggested: psychoecology, ecotherapy, global therapy, green therapy, Earth-centered therapy, reearthing, nature-based psychotherapy, shamanic counseling, even sylvan therapy...By whatever name, the underlying assumption is the same: *ecology needs psychology, psychology needs ecology*. The context for defining sanity in our time has reached planetary magnitude (*Where Psyche Meets Gaia* section of *Ecopsychology: Restoring the Earth; Healing the Mind*, pp. 4-5).

xviii Mark Schroll follows the path of ecopsychology and the conception of ecopsychology from Fox and the deep ecology movement, to Robert Greenway (who called the field of study psychoecology) when Roszak attended discussion groups related to the topic in 1990. Through his postings in the Ecopsychology group on Facebook I find him to be always be the historian. The work I'm referencing to here is 29 in References Chapter 1.

xix In wilderness, we begin to develop a sustained continuum of mindfulness...We are invited to observe with attentiveness what emerges around each bend of the trail, what unfolds before us over each hill....We are...attentively aware of wherever our awareness flows (*The Way of Wilderness* from *Ecopsychology: Restoring the Earth, Healing the Mind*, p. 189).

xx The core of the mind is the ecological unconscious. For ecopsychology, repression of the ecological unconscious is the deepest root of collusive madness in industrial society; open access to the ecological unconscious is the path to sanity (*The Voice of the Earth*, p. 320).

xxi The modern world's pathological suppression of our innate ecological connectedness begins from the moment of birth. It occurs in the commonplace practice of separating the infant from the mother...The traumatic separation breaks the physical "continuum" between mother and child (*The Voice of the Earth*, p. 301).

xxii By adapting gradually to the loss of actual nature and to the increase of technological nature, humans will lower the baseline across generations for what counts as a full measure of the human experience and of human flourishing (*The Human Relation with Nature* in the *Association for Psychological Science*, p. 37).

xxiii Resilience is something that may be very hard to see, unless you exceed its limits, overwhelm and damage the balancing loops, and the system structure breaks down. Because resilience may not be obvious without a whole-system view, people often sacrifice resilience for stability, or for productivity, or for some other more immediately recognizable system property (*Thinking in Systems*, p. 77).

xxiv This is a summary of the story told on pages 230-231 in *Shouting at the Sky* (2009).

xxv The dangerous, bold, risk- taking energies of youth are necessary for an initiatory process to take place, as all primal cultures know. Ours does not. Primal societies use these energies to mediate that great transition of each generation from dependence to independence, from immaturity to maturity, from childhood to adulthood, for the sustaining of the community both materially and spiritually (*Is the Modern Psyche Undergoing a Rite of Passage?*, pp. 17-18).

xxvi Although distantly related to the dog, the bear is a closer relative to the raccoon (*Animal Speak*, p. 252).

xxvii A number of animals were considered particularly sacred to Artemis. Chief amongst these were the deer, the dog and the bear, but they also included the boar, the hare and possibly the lion. Several birds were also considered sacred to her, including the partridge, quail and buzzard (*Artemis: Virgin Goddess of the Sun, Moon, & Hunt*, ebook location 2557-2560).

xxviii The bear was especially sacred to Artemis, both as the creature and also as the stellar constellation of Ursa Major, the Great Bear. Killing her sacred bears was the most certain way of bringing down Artemis' wrath (*Artemis: Virgin Goddess of the Sun, Moon, & Hunt*, ebook location 2565-2567).

xxix We were three scientists who had been requested to explain the current understanding of climate change and the role that humans might have in causing global warming…The president's refusal to sign on to Kyoto was expected. More important was the revelation on March 13 that the United States would not regulate carbon dioxide emissions from power plants. That decision was a heavy blow to environmentalists and scientists who realized that Earth's climate was approaching a dangerous situation because of the buildup of atmospheric carbon dioxide (*Storms of my Grandchildren,* pp. 1, 2).

xxx Psychotherapy is perhaps one of the few commercial businesses that doesn't see itself as one, that views financial gain as unseemly when connected to the delicate work of emotional insight (*What Brand is Your Therapist* from the *New York Times*).

xxxi Accepting and living by sufficiency rather than excess offers a return to...the ancient order of family, community, good work, and good life; to a reverence for skill, creativity, and creation; to a daily cadence slow enough to let us watch the sunset and stroll by the water's edge; to communities worth spending a lifetime in; and to local places pregnant with the memories of generations (*Are We Happy Yet* of *Ecopsychology,* p. 76)

xxxii Joseph Campbell: A young Sioux boy around nine years old...became sick, psychologically sick...The family is terribly concerned about it, and they send for a shaman who has had the experience in his own youth, to come as a kind of psychoanalyst and pull the youngster out of it. But instead of relieving the boy of the deities, the shaman is adapting him to the deities and the deities to himself. It's a different problem from psychoanalysis. I think it was Nietzsche who said, "Be careful lest in casting out the devils you cast out the best thing that's in you." (*The Power of Myth,* p. 110)